DAVID'S
HAMMER

THE CASE FOR AN ACTIVIST JUDICIARY

CLINT BOLICK

CATO
INSTITUTE
WASHINGTON, D.C.

The Cato Institute gratefully acknowledges the generous contribution of Steve G. Stevanovich to the production of this book.

Library of Congress Cataloging-in-Publication Data

Bolick, Clint.
    David's hammer : the case for an activist judiciary / Clint Bolick.
        p. cm.
    Includes bibliographical references and index.
    ISBN 978-1-933995-03-8 (cloth : alk. paper)
    ISBN 978-1-933995-02-1 (paper : alk. paper)
        1. Political questions and judicial power—United States. I. Title.

    KF384.B58 2007
    347.73′1—dc22

                                                          2007060887

Cover design by Jon Meyers.

Printed in the United States of America.

CATO INSTITUTE
1000 Massachusetts Ave., N.W.
Washington, D.C. 20001
www.cato.org

DAVID'S
HAMMER

For Kali Aspen Bolick

Contents

Foreword

I suspect that a lot of people will see the subtitle of this book and instinctively decide that they disagree with what is inside (although I hope it will prompt them to pick up the book and read it). That is because "judicial activism" today is the universal pejorative, the one thing that liberals and conservatives agree is wrong, even if they disagree over what it is.

Who on Earth possibly could stand up for judicial activism? The moniker conjures images of imperious jurists in marble temples sitting in judgment on matters rightly consigned to democratic processes, bereft of constitutional constraint and subject only to their own hubristic whims.

Indeed, over the past 75 years or so, we have seen abundant examples of precisely that type of judicial arrogance, in which judges literally invent new constitutional or statutory rights out of thin air, exercise sweeping powers that belong to other branches of government, and act as if completely unbound to any type of constitutional moorings. Such examples of judicial activism—or, more accurately, as my friend Gene Meyer suggests, "judicial lawlessness"—deserve contempt, for they do extreme damage to the integrity of the judiciary and to the rule of law that undergirds a free society.

But increasingly, many today on both the right and the left define judicial activism in simpler terms, as the act of courts striking down laws enacted by the democratic branches. Thus defined, and still cast in a pejorative manner, the term suggests that courts ought routinely to defer to the elected branches of government (or, for that matter, to the many unelected officials who actually create and apply most of the laws and regulations that govern us today).

To the notion, clothed in that conventional wisdom, that judges ought to defer to the elected branches of government, this book posits two questions: why and to what effect? Americans do not live in a pure democracy where the majority rules, much less where powerful and highly motivated special interests are entitled to manipulate government powers to their own ends. We live in a constitutional republic. The overarching principle of our system of government is that all of its constituents—the executive, legislative, and judicial branches as well as the people themselves—are bound by the Constitution. The primary goal of that Constitution is to protect freedom. And within that system, for better or worse, the courts are assigned the role of keeping the other branches of government within the assigned limits of their constitutional powers.

Given the explosive growth of government at every level and the resulting erosion of freedom, the problem with judicial activism thus defined is not too much of it but too little. In assessing the constitutionality of laws and regulations, regardless how oppressive, the courts indulge a presumption of constitutionality. Through procedural rules, they have judged many laws and regulations to be essentially nonreviewable. Worst of all, they have excised from our Constitution precious liberties and limitations on government power that the founders rightly believed were essential to American liberty.

I'm biased. I have spent most of my career challenging government laws and regulations in court. I chose the courts in which to operate for two principal reasons: in the courts an advocate can achieve outcomes that are painted in black and white, rather than shades of gray; and courts are a forum in which the proverbial David can, and often does, defeat Goliath (hence the title of the book). My cases (many of which are described in the pages that follow) have involved real people fighting for their rights against oppressive government. Typically, those people cannot vindicate their rights in the political arena, where the odds simply are too stacked against the little guy. But they often can and do win in court, because the judicial mandate, properly construed, is to apply the rule of law to the facts without regard to the resources or political clout of the litigants.

I hope that in the following pages I can convince readers that judicial protection of individual rights exists not too much but far too little, and moreover, that judges can and should be bound by a set of principles that would prevent judicial lawlessness while still allowing the courts to carry out their vital role of safeguarding freedom.

Along the way, I write about both judicial misadventures and triumphs. I begin with one of my own cases, which challenged regulatory barriers to interstate shipment of wine to consumers, and which sparked a spirited debate (no pun intended) over the proper exercise of judicial authority. I then turn to arguments made by critics of judicial activism on both the right and the left, some of which are valid and others that would eviscerate the vital role of the judiciary in the protection of individual liberty. From there I address what the Constitution's Framers had in mind when they created a federal judiciary, and I trace the uneven record of the U.S. Supreme Court in fulfilling its intended role, emphasizing the Warren and Rehnquist Courts. Through cases affecting individual rights and the limits of government power, I examine the sharply varying real-world implications of courts that take their constitutional duties seriously and those that do not. I end by exploring briefly the largely untapped potential of state courts in interpreting their own constitutions to protect individual liberty and constrain government power.

I have focused mainly on domestic constitutional issues. Two important areas I have not covered extensively because of my lack of expertise are criminal law and national security, the latter of which has become increasingly important after the terrorist attacks on September 11, 2001. Those issues concern me greatly, but I leave it to others to flesh out the proper boundaries of judicial intervention in those areas. As my discussion of wartime powers during World War II indicates, however, I do not believe that constitutional liberties should be suspended in time of war, which is when they often are most tested. Such concerns are particularly implicated when the war is undeclared and waged against largely unknown foes for an uncertain duration. Had I included criminal and national security issues, I suspect that some of the justices who in my analysis do not fare well on other issues might fare better overall, and vice versa. The ideal judge, however, is one who broadly interprets both constitutional liberties and limits on government power, regardless of the context.

I am enormously grateful to the Cato Institute for publishing this book and especially to David Boaz, Bob Levy, and Roger Pilon for their excellent editing and enthusiasm for the project. I am appreciative as well to my former colleagues at the Institute for Justice for their support, good work, and inspiration and to my clients over the years for their heroism. After three years as president and general counsel of the Alliance for School Choice, I am returning to the vineyards of litigation (metaphor intended), and this book sketches a bit of what I hope is the realm of the possible for a freedom-oriented litigation practice. In the meantime, I hope this book will spark debate that focuses less on overheated, partisan rhetoric and more on the nature and role of the institutions that are necessary to preserve freedom in our great nation.

—Clint Bolick
Phoenix, Arizona
August 2006

1. Mrs. Swedenburg Goes to Court

The Constitution is not neutral. It was designed to take the government off the backs of the people.

—Justice William O. Douglas[1]

From the beginning of my legal education, law for me has been intertwined with wine. Fittingly, my first U.S. Supreme Court argument was about the beverage that is the sublime joint product of nature and human ingenuity.

The case of Juanita Swedenburg, a proud woman, a farmer and entrepreneur who asks nothing of her government but to be left alone to mind her own business, is emblematic of the debate over the role of the judiciary in a free society. For when all else failed in Mrs. Swedenburg's quest to pursue her livelihood free from arbitrary government interference, she did what many Americans do when their basic rights are violated: she turned to the courts for justice. Whether the courts should help ordinary Americans like Juanita Swedenburg or should leave them to the mercy of democratic politics, even when politics are dominated by powerful special interests, is at the heart of the debate over what is pejoratively called "judicial activism."

For better or worse, the task of resolving such important matters is largely in the hands of lawyers. Law, as William Shakespeare understood, is not always the noblest of professions. Many lawyers make their living off the misfortunes and disputes of others. It is, for most, a mercenary profession: lawyers take their clients as they find them; they are obliged to zealously represent them; and winning, rather than justice, is the goal of most litigation. Lawyers draft the laws that make society so complex that lawyers are needed even for the simplest transactions; then lawyers make the simplest transactions so complex that lawyers are needed to decipher and, in the end, litigate them. The American legal system, designed of course by lawyers, is rigged so that even the most frivolous claims

1

entail little risk for the lawyers pursuing them; indeed, the cost of defending against litigation is so great that "voluntary" settlements, which invariably entail a payoff to the lawyer prosecuting the action, are routine. Those costs are then passed along to all of us in the form of higher prices and fewer choices.[2] Law is often such a racket that sharks are said to never attack a lawyer because of professional courtesy.

Most Americans seem to share my disdain for the legal profession as a whole. Among American professions requiring a doctorate, lawyers alone are deemed not entitled to use the "doctor" honorific, substituting instead the quaint term "esquire" following the name. By contrast, when I visit Germany, I am greeted as "Herr Doktor Professor" Bolick—a double honorific!—suggesting that at least in some countries, lawyers are deemed worthy of special respect. I'm not sure that idea would go over very well in our country.

And yet, as cynical as the legal system and profession can be, American law also has a romantic aspect. For all its flaws, law in a free society is the most powerful tool to correct injustice. In no other system in the world can the low so readily bring the mighty to account. In our nation, the courtroom is the great equalizer. A creative lawyer can change the world in one fell swoop. That was what the Framers of our constitutional experiment intended, for they understood that courts were necessary to provide the ultimate check against tyrannical government. Whatever maladies courts might visit upon American society, they continue to play that liberty-enhancing role today. Our judiciary is at once both a legacy of and prerequisite for our enduring free society.

I experienced that revelation during college. I had prepared for a career in teaching and politics. As I neared graduation, however, I discovered that neither profession was suited to an idealist. Our public education system, even in the late 1970s, was in serious decline; it required systemic change, which was not achievable one student at a time. My experiences with politics, both local and national, suggested that principle was, to say the least, not the foremost consideration. At best, compromise in a forward direction seemed possible, but not sweeping change.

As I was discovering all that, I was also taking an undergraduate course in constitutional law. As the son of a welder whose formal education never went beyond eighth grade, I'm not sure I had ever even met a lawyer, and like most Americans, I held the legal profession in disdain. I took the course hesitantly, mainly because of the reputation of its teacher, Robert G. Smith, the esteemed Drew University professor emeritus of political science. Reading about cases such as *Brown v. Board of Education* was an epiphany: law used as the Framers intended could work revolutionary change in our society, bringing down systems of oppression such as the separate-but-equal regimes. Unlike politicians, lawyers arguing in the courts can hold fast to underlying principles and achieve change without compromise. The appeal was alluring, and before I knew it my Volkswagen Dasher was packed with all of my belongings on a cross-country trek to law school at the University of California at Davis.

Davis proved to be a harsh environment. Diversity was encouraged in everything except philosophical viewpoints. Having experienced a true liberal arts environment at Drew, I was astounded at the ideological homogeneity and hostility that permeated Davis. So I took my New Jersey palate to the nearby Napa Valley and found frequent sweet refuge in the head-spinning assortment of wines. The free tastings were perfect for a poor student's budget. And when my classmates in their collective wisdom chose Ralph Nader as our commencement speaker (after all, Jane Fonda, who had spoken previously, was a tough act to follow), I celebrated my liberation instead with my family in the more congenial surroundings of the Napa vineyards.

Armed with a law degree and somehow having managed to convince the California legal cartel that I was fit to practice, I immediately began suing bureaucrats for a living. Nine years later, in 1991, I cofounded the Institute for Justice (IJ) in Washington, D.C., with Chip Mellor. Many of the cases my IJ colleagues and I litigated are discussed in the following pages. Until I left IJ in 2004 to work full-time for school choice, I often said that my colleagues and I had the greatest jobs in the legal profession: we got to choose our cases, choose our clients, and not charge anything for our representation. Best of all, the people we sued were bureaucrats.

Although my interest in wine persisted as I embarked upon my legal career, some time passed before that passion dovetailed with my work. My curiosity was sparked, however, during a visit in the early 1990s to a small winery in bucolic Middleburg, Virginia. The proprietor was a striking older woman, Juanita Swedenburg, who owned and operated the winery with her husband. She produced several good wines, including a chardonnay with the toastiest nose I can remember. We got to talking, and Mrs. Swedenburg asked me what I did for a living. When I told her that, among other things, I challenged regulatory barriers to entrepreneurship, she exclaimed, "Have I got a regulation for you!"

Most states, it turned out, prohibited direct interstate shipments of wine to consumers. Thus, if tourists from another state visited Mrs. Swedenburg's winery and asked how they could obtain her wines back home, she would have to reply, "You can't." The only way Mrs. Swedenburg could sell her wines in other states would be to obtain a distributor, and most distributors have little interest in handling a few cases from an obscure Virginia winery. Nor was Mrs. Swedenburg inclined to hand over 30 percent of the retail price to a distributor who added nothing of value. For all practical purposes, Mrs. Swedenburg's small business was shut out of the market outside her home state.

As a descendant of settlers who fought in the American Revolution, Mrs. Swedenburg was outraged that such a stupid law could exist in a nation with the greatest free-enterprise system in the world. I wondered too. Indeed, the problem seemed widespread: I knew obtaining wines from some of my favorite small wineries in California was difficult. Virginia, it turns out, allowed direct shipment to consumers of wine produced within the state but not from wineries outside its borders.

But it would be several years before I could turn my attention to challenging the laws. I was extremely busy with other cases, and I knew my colleagues at IJ would greet with skepticism any case I proposed involving wine. I would have to demonstrate that some bigger principle was at stake than my passion for wine. Most of the cases at IJ involved states' imposing oppressive restraints upon their own citizens, which we challenged under the Fourteenth Amendment; the wine issue, by contrast, presented a trade barrier erected by some states against entrepreneurs in other states. In the meantime, I had to avoid Mrs. Swedenburg's winery lest she ask me why I wasn't taking on her legal albatross.

When finally I had a chance to turn my attention to the issue of direct interstate shipment of wines, I found that indeed a bigger principle was involved: freedom of commerce among the states, whose protection was one of the principal motivations for creating the U.S. Constitution. Under the Articles of Confederation, states were locked in debilitating trade wars. To protect their own industries, states would shut off imports from other states. If such actions persisted, the United States never would constitute a single economic union, which, in turn, would inhibit its prosperity. The Framers of the Constitution saw clearly that the states could not be trusted to resist protectionist temptations and that the remedy would be to confer authority upon Congress to regulate trade, thereby preventing states from enacting parochial trade barriers that impeded the national interest in free domestic trade. That understanding took the form of article I, section 8, of the Constitution, which delegated to Congress the exclusive authority to "regulate Commerce . . . among the several States."

Those few words, that seemingly simple command, have given rise to much of the debate over judicial activism during the past 75 years. The overarching question, one that I will touch upon later, is whether the Framers, in giving Congress the authority to regulate commerce, meant to limit that power to commerce or rather to allow Congress to regulate everything. Given that the latter construction not only ignores the plain meaning of the clause but also fundamentally transforms the Constitution from a charter of limited and defined powers into an open-ended grant of plenary national authority, the answer to the question seems obvious. But apparently it is not, as we shall see.

The question raised in the wine context was a different and also recurring one: what happens if the states enact trade barriers but Congress does not exercise its authority to regulate commerce in a given instance? In the face of congressional silence, may states create protectionist trade barriers? In other words, is affirmative congressional action necessary to effectuate the core purpose of the commerce clause, or is the clause self-executing so as to prohibit state-erected protectionist trade barriers of its own accord? The doctrine that the commerce clause by its own terms prohibits such trade barriers is referred to as the "dormant" or "negative" commerce clause.

This is the stuff of many a scholarly debate and so may make the eyes of mere mortals glaze over. Yet the answers to that question—

like the answer to so many seemingly arcane questions of constitutional law—are of utmost importance to the likes of Juanita Swedenburg. And not to her alone. More than two centuries after ratification of the Constitution, states *still* cannot resist the temptation to distort markets to benefit their own domestic industries to the detriment of out-of-state competitors. So that, as if to demonstrate the prescience of the Framers, the constitutional guarantee of free trade in the Internet era is perhaps even more vital than it was in the founding era.

That is because of the Internet's revolutionary power of "disintermediation"—the ability of producers and consumers to meet and transact business in cyberspace, without the necessity, or added cost and inconvenience, of a middleman. In this way, the Internet is the greatest agent of consumer freedom in the history of mankind.

And yet, as *Star Wars* teaches, the Empire always strikes back. Some middlemen have adapted to and flourished in the Internet era. But others have resorted to the age-old tradition of seeking government protection against competition and innovation. Businesses selling products ranging from insurance to automobiles to contact lenses to caskets have flocked to their state legislatures to restrict or prohibit transactions over the Internet, thus preserving their economic hegemony and limiting consumer choices.[3]

That was the situation with wine. Over the past few decades, the number of American wineries has grown to approximately 3,000 in all 50 states—the overwhelming majority of them small, family-run enterprises that produce only 2,000 or 3,000 cases each year. At the same time, the liquor-distributor industry experienced extreme consolidation, so that today a handful of behemoths dominate the multibillion-dollar industry. As a result, the distributors can distribute only a fraction of the tens of thousands of distinct wines produced each year in our nation alone. By contrast, the Internet offers the potential that middlemen cannot for matching consumers with their favorite wines, no matter how vast the choices.

Bans on direct shipment of wine are a relic of the post-Prohibition era, when states wanted to stifle organized crime by separating the production of alcohol from its distribution. They created mandatory "three-tier" systems of alcohol distribution: producer to distributor to retailer. In the unique context of wine, however, a number of states, eager to promote their own wine production, acted to allow

direct shipping from in-state wineries. To protect in-state distributors, however, many states also acted to forbid shipping by out-of-
state wineries directly to consumers. When IJ filed a lawsuit against
New York in 1999 on behalf of Juanita Swedenburg, 31 states prohibited direct interstate wine shipments to consumers. Seven of them
made such shipments a felony. The discriminatory trade barriers
presented a textbook example of precisely the evil that the Framers
intended to forbid when they placed the commerce clause in the
Constitution.

The Federal Trade Commission studied the issue and found that
"State bans on interstate direct shipping represent the single largest
regulatory barrier to expanded e-commerce in wine."[4] The states'
professed regulatory concerns—protecting against underage access
to alcohol and tax collection—all could be facilitated, the commission
found, through regulatory actions short of discriminatory prohibitions against direct shipping.

The trade barriers raised the question of the scope of the "dormant" commerce clause, which in reality has never been dormant.
Decades of cases have found that where a state regulates commerce
not by one set of rules but by two—one regulatory regime that
applies to out-of-state products and another, less-onerous regime
for domestic products—the burden shifts to the state to demonstrate
a compelling state interest that cannot be achieved through less-
burdensome means.[5] By that rule of law, many discriminatory trade
barriers have been struck down over the years—effectuating the
Framers' desire to ensure a free national market.

That doctrine likely would have resolved the matter in Juanita
Swedenburg's favor if she were selling a product other than alcohol.
But another constitutional provision—the Twenty-First Amendment, which repealed Prohibition—pertains directly to alcohol. That
amendment prohibits the "transportation or importation into any
State . . . for delivery or use therein of intoxicating liquors, in violation of the laws thereof."

For some, those words began and ended the debate. Where prohibited by state law, direct shipping of wine unquestionably encompassed the "transportation or importation" of "intoxicating liquors"
into a state "in violation of the laws thereof." Therefore, some would
argue that regardless of a state's motivation, its alcohol laws are
protected by the Twenty-First Amendment.

7

Nevertheless, no Constitution would have existed for the Twenty-First Amendment to amend were it not for the constitutional guarantee of national economic union. The Twenty-First Amendment did not repeal the commerce clause. When faced with seemingly competing constitutional provisions, the proper role of courts, my colleagues and I argued, was to harmonize the two provisions, not to aggrandize one while draining the other of meaning.

The surface conflict between the commerce clause and the Twenty-First Amendment also raised a more fundamental question lurking beneath much constitutional litigation: is the Constitution a grant of government power to which rights are the exception or a recognition of individual rights to which government power is the exception? When faced with a dispute between an asserted freedom and an asserted government power, should a court indulge a presumption in favor of government power or individual liberty?[6] The answer to that threshold question of constitutional interpretation would affect not only Juanita Swedenburg but also scores of other people whose rights are restricted by government power.

For some, the questions raised by the direct-shipping issue were quite easy. The first appellate judge to rule on the issue was Frank Easterbrook of the U.S. Court of Appeals for the Seventh Circuit, a jurist who does not lack for self-assurance. Like many conservatives, Easterbrook doubts the doctrine that the commerce clause on its own accord prohibits protectionist trade barriers. For Easterbrook, the question presented was one of states' rights, which should triumph because Congress had not exercised its regulatory authority to prevent state regulation. In upholding Indiana's direct-shipment ban, the opening words of Judge Easterbrook's opinion clearly forecast the outcome: "This case pits the twenty-first amendment, which appears in the Constitution, against the 'dormant commerce clause,' which does not."[7]

For others, the question was not so simple. The leading U.S. Supreme Court precedent was a 1984 case, *Bacchus Imports v. Dias*, in which the Court struck down a Hawaii law that exempted certain liquors produced in state from an otherwise applicable alcohol tax. The obvious purpose was to benefit domestic producers. (Ironically, the same Frank Easterbrook who later as a judge would disdain the dormant commerce clause argued the *Bacchus* case successfully for the challengers.) The *Bacchus* Court harmonized the commerce clause and the Twenty-First Amendment, noting that although the amendment's scope was broad: "One thing is certain: The central purpose of the [Twenty-First Amendment] was not to empower states to benefit local liquor industries by erecting barriers to economic competition." For that reason, the Court held, "State laws that constitute mere economic protectionism are . . . not entitled to the same deference as laws enacted to combat the perceived evils of an unrestricted traffic in liquor."[8] So if the courts applied *Bacchus,* the question in our case would be whether the state's ban addressed "the perceived evils of an unrestricted traffic in liquor" or whether in reality it constituted "mere economic protectionism."

The wine cases were characterized by remarkable cross-ideological alliances on both sides. On our side were prominent conservatives such as Kenneth Starr and Barbara Olson; on the other side, conservatives included Robert Bork, C. Boyden Gray, and Miguel Estrada. Our "free the grapes" legal team also included such liberal stalwarts as former Stanford Law School dean Kathleen Sullivan and University of Indiana lawyer Alex Tanford, who frequently litigated cases for the American Civil Liberties Union and was a debate opponent of mine on the school-choice issue. Conservative jurists, such as Judge Easterbrook of the Seventh Circuit and Richard Wesley of the Second Circuit, reached opposite conclusions from other conservatives, such as J. Michael Luttig of the Fourth Circuit and Danny Boggs of the Sixth Circuit; liberal judges such as Sonia Sotomayor of the Second Circuit were at variance with other liberal judges, such as Martha Daughtrey of the Sixth Circuit. Never before had I litigated an issue that transcended ideological boundaries as dramatically as this one did. Yet sharp lines of rhetorical demarcation existed: judicial "activism" versus judicial "restraint," and "states' rights" versus the supremacy of the federal Constitution and national economic union.

Although several cases raising similar legal claims would be litigated by various advocates en route to the U.S. Supreme Court, my colleagues and I decided to challenge New York's law. We chose New York for two major reasons: after California, New York's wine market is the largest in the United States, and its direct-shipment laws discriminated in favor of New York wineries and against out-of-state wineries. Notably, almost all of the New York wineries supported our lawsuit: although they enjoyed sheltered markets in

9

New York, they were shut out from direct shipping to other states in retaliation for New York's ban on direct out-of-state shipping.

In challenging the New York regime, we were taking on the big boys. No sooner did we file our lawsuit than seven powerful interests intervened to help defend the law: the state's four largest liquor distributors, whose combined revenues exceeded one billion dollars annually; the package stores, which enjoyed a monopoly over the retail sale of interstate wine; the truckers' union, which enjoyed a monopoly over wine delivery; and the Rev. Calvin Butts, who was concerned about underage access. Not all of the interests on the other side seemed entirely savory: the press reported that around the time of our lawsuit, 50 Federal Bureau of Investigation agents raided one of the liquor distributors seeking evidence of mob connections. The massive orchestrated special-interest intervention in our case suggested that New York was the chosen field of battle in which the liquor-distributor behemoth would take its stand.

The New York litigation made for unusual adversaries as well. The lead lawyer for the liquor distributors was Randy Mastro, a prominent New York lawyer who had served as deputy mayor under Rudolph Giuliani. On our side as an expert was John Dyson, a businessman who owned wineries in Italy, New York, and California, and who was another Giuliani deputy mayor. Adding to the ironies was that Mastro's late father had been a political science professor of mine at Drew University and frequently had urged that some day I needed to work with Randy. When I met Randy, who bears an uncanny physical resemblance to his dad, I told him I didn't think that this encounter was what his father had in mind. The high-priced, big-firm lawyers on the other side tended to be the types who judged other attorneys by their hourly rates. Given that my colleagues and I at IJ charged our clients nothing, I can only imagine the disdain in which our adversary lawyers held us.

The quality and temperament of a judge can make all the difference in a case. We were very fortunate that the judge assigned to us was Richard Berman, an appointee of President Bill Clinton who was bright, courteous, thoughtful, thorough, and judicious. During our first court hearing, my colleague from IJ and I were literally surrounded in a semi-circle by a phalanx of 18 lawyers representing the combined interests on the other side. Judge Berman smiled when I likened it to David versus Goliath. In subsequent hearings, most of our opposing lawyers sat discreetly in the gallery, but the image was indelibly established.

Throughout the trial-court litigation, the lawyer for the state barely made a peep, ceding the law's defense to the liquor distributors' lawyers. They in turn litigated the case with such bombast and hyperbole that it would have driven me crazy if I had not grown up among similar personalities in neighboring New Jersey. The spectacle of the liquor distributors' tail wagging the state's dog was enormously helpful to us in demonstrating that the purpose and effect of the laws were protectionism, not public health and safety.

That was the case we put on. We showed that the original three-tier system was adopted at the behest of the liquor distributors. When the legislature in the 1990s overwhelmingly passed direct-shipping legislation, the liquor distributors urged Governor George Pataki to veto it, and he did, citing concerns for domestic industry and tax revenues. As for underage consumption, we produced state records showing that the relevant numbers were 16,000 and zero—the first being the number of reported instances of minors' obtaining alcohol through the three-tier system over a five-year period; the second being the reported instances of minors' obtaining alcohol over the Internet during the same period. I told the judge that if my college-age son could navigate the system by ordering wine over the Internet using a credit card, satisfying the winery that he was over 21, arranging to accept delivery on campus of a box labeled "Alcohol: Adult Identification Required," and producing another acceptable identification upon delivery, I would celebrate his ingenuity with him over a glass of cabernet. Unfortunately, the existing system allows minors far too many ways to obtain alcohol for them to have to resort to the far more cumbersome process of ordering it over the Internet. Ultimately, our case rested on the logic that whatever rules applied to deliveries to consumers by in-state wineries ought to apply also to deliveries by out-of-state wineries; the fact that two sets of rules applied rather than one demonstrated that the purpose and effect of the laws were protectionist.

Our adversaries relied heavily on the underage access issue, offering evidence that states with permissive direct-shipping laws also reported higher rates of binge drinking on college campuses. (It was hard to imagine college students guzzling Mrs. Swedenburg's chardonnay at a keg party, but maybe kids have become more sophisticated since my college years.) Without a shred of irony, the liquor distributors joined forces with Christian conservatives and groups committed to alcohol abstinence. The distributors argued that state authority under the Twenty-First Amendment was plenary and that Congress had affirmatively given states the power to ban direct interstate shipping.

Judge Berman didn't buy it. "That the New York direct shipping ban on out-of-state wine burdens interstate commerce and is discriminatory (on its face) is clear," he ruled.[9] Moreover, he found that "the direct shipping ban was designed to protect New York State businesses from out-of-state competition."[10] Applying the *Bacchus* decision, he concluded that the Twenty-First Amendment provided no shelter because the "State has not established that its goals cannot be accomplished in a nondiscriminatory manner."[11] As a result, he ordered that the state allow out-of-state direct shipment of wine on the same terms and conditions as in-state direct shipping.

The liquor-distributor empire quickly struck back, filing an appeal in the U.S. Court of Appeals for the Second Circuit. That court reached a starkly different result on states' rights grounds. Recognizing that a majority of the Second Circuit's sister courts had ruled in favor of challenges to discriminatory wine shipment bans, Judge Richard Wesley found that those decisions had "the effect of unnecessarily limiting the authority delegated to the states" under the Twenty-First Amendment.[12] Moreover, the court found that no real discrimination took place, for "all wineries, whether in-state or out-of-state, are permitted to obtain a license as long as the winery establishes a physical presence in the state."[13] The state's interest, in reality, was not protectionism but in ensuring "accountability," which could be accomplished by requiring a physical presence of all wineries.

The "physical presence" requirement sounded benign—who could object to a business establishing a physical presence in the state in order to ensure "accountability" to the state's legitimate regulatory regime? In practice, however, that jurisprudential innovation could have created the exception that would have swallowed the commerce clause. A small winemaker like Juanita Swedenburg would have found opening and fully staffing a warehouse just to gain the privilege of selling a few cases of wine in New York economically impossible. Multiply that burden by 50, if other states followed suit, and the rule would close markets to small wineries all across the United States. The decision boded chilling ramifications far beyond wine: if every state could require a physical presence upon the pretense of health or safety concerns, the vast promise of the Internet to expand consumer freedom would halt in its tracks. After all, the whole point of the commerce clause was that an enterprise in one state could do business in another state without having to move there. The state's legitimate regulatory interests with regard to alcohol could be achieved in less onerous fashion, such as requiring a license in order to do business. Indeed, federal law provides plenty of potent tools to enforce state alcohol laws against out-of-state companies.

Because the Second Circuit decision conflicted with decisions from other circuits, prospects for review by the U.S. Supreme Court looked promising. But once the high court took the case—along with a companion case from Michigan, in which the trial court had upheld the direct-shipment ban but the appeals court had struck it down—the prospects didn't seem especially encouraging. Although we had the leading precedent on our side, 20 years had passed since the *Bacchus* decision. In that time, all five of the justices in the majority were gone, while the three dissenters (Chief Justice William H. Rehnquist and Justices John Paul Stevens and Sandra Day O'Connor) were still on the Court. Moreover, Justice Thomas believes no such thing as the dormant commerce clause exists and the rights often protected under that doctrine in fact were intended to be protected under other constitutional provisions.[14] We tried to attract Justice Thomas's vote by including a separate claim under the privileges and immunities clause of article IV, section 2, of the Constitution, whose scope largely mirrors the commerce clause, but the Court did not accept review on that issue.

So we assumed that we began our trek to the U.S. Supreme Court with four likely votes against us and no certain votes in favor. If our math was correct, we would need to cobble together the votes of Justices Anthony Kennedy, Antonin Scalia, David Souter, Ruth Bader Ginsburg, and Stephen Breyer—an odd-couple lineup that apparently never had been previously aligned in a 5-4 decision.

The uncertain endurance of the *Bacchus* decision allowed our opponents to return to basics and argue that state power under the Twenty-First Amendment was plenary. A "plain language" and

13

states' rights approach might appeal to Justice Scalia and tip the balance against us. We countered with a strong historical analysis showing that the Twenty-First Amendment had merely restored the status quo prior to Prohibition—and that discrimination and protectionism were not encompassed within the states' powers to regulate alcohol at that time. We also had the benefit of a strong record of protectionism in the New York case and of the Federal Trade Commission report that laid waste to the states' defenses relating to underage access and taxation.

While the case headed toward argument before the Supreme Court, both sides made their cases in the court of public opinion. State attorneys general launched high-profile sting operations ostensibly to demonstrate how easy it was for underage buyers to game the system. (Revealingly, the sting artists never ordered successfully from wineries, but from retailers, who were licensed by the three-tier system yet avoided its regulations.) On our side, the feisty and highly quotable Juanita Swedenburg was the poster-child small entrepreneur fighting for her right to earn an honest living. As the argument approached, Mrs. Swedenburg's husband and business partner, Wayne, passed away, depriving her of a major source of strength and support. But if her determination ever flagged, I never saw it.

In our side's oral argument, former Stanford Law School dean Kathleen Sullivan argued the Michigan case, and I represented the New York plaintiffs. To buttress their states' rights argument, New York and Michigan jettisoned the liquor distributors' lawyers, who had done the heavy lifting in the earlier rounds, in favor of the solicitors general from the two states. But the move didn't work, because the states' lawyers insisted that their powers under the Twenty-First Amendment were without limit, essentially asking the Court to overrule *Bacchus*. Even Justice O'Connor, who had dissented in *Bacchus*, seemed taken aback by the states' extreme position. For my part, I pointed out the heavy influence of protectionism in New York's regulatory scheme and assailed the "presence" requirement. Were the justices to visit Swedenburg Winery (which I cheerfully encouraged them to do), they could find Mrs. Swedenburg harvesting grapes, tending the tasting room, bottling wine, and filling orders. The thought that she could afford to open a New York operation in order to sell a few cases of wine there was ludicrous.

In the end, the Court divided 5-4 in striking down the discriminatory Michigan and New York laws. Justice Kennedy, writing for the majority that included Justices Scalia, Souter, Ginsburg, and Breyer, declared that the effect of the laws was "to allow in-state wineries to sell wine directly to consumers in that State but to prohibit out-of-state wineries from doing so, or, at the least, to make direct sales impractical from an economic standpoint."[15] Such laws, the Court ruled, "deprive citizens of their right to have access to the markets of other States on equal terms."[16] The Court flatly rejected the physical presence defense, remarking that "for most wineries, the expense of establishing a bricks-and-mortar distribution operation in 1 State, let alone all 50, is prohibitive."[17] Nor did the Court credit the states' underage access or taxation arguments, finding that less-onerous alternatives were available to service legitimate state interests. The Court's legal holding was simple—"state regulation of alcohol is limited by the nondiscrimination principle of the Commerce Clause"[18]—and the New York and Michigan laws violated that principle, with no convincing justification.

For Mrs. Swedenburg, the victory was sweet vindication. As fate would have it, although I spoke to her the day the decision came down, I didn't actually get to see her until months later, whereupon I received what must have been the biggest hug of my entire life.

The case was a vindication of the American legal system as well. In few other nations could one small entrepreneur prevail over the powerful combination of massive commercial interests and government. Her triumph demonstrates that ours truly is a nation governed by the rule of law.

Indeed, that spectacle—the judicial redress of injustice visited upon an individual by the government—is a hallmark of a free society. By contrast, the *New York Times* recently profiled the failed attempts of Chinese citizens to challenge oppressive laws, years after the legal system in Communist China ostensibly was changed to allow such actions.[19] That Americans can bring down tyrannical laws through peaceful judicial action, while people in many other countries cannot, is testimony that ours remains among the freest nations in the world.

Yet plainly, not everyone would agree that such judicial power is a positive phenomenon. The legal clash in the direct-shipping cases between the small wineries and the liquor distributors is a microcosm of the debate over the proper role of the courts in the American constitutional system. Those who assert that courts should defer to democratic processes would consign the likes of Juanita Swedenburg to defeat and despair, while rendering a nullity the constitutional promise of freedom of commerce. There is no way that Juanita Swedenburg could take on the powerful liquor distributors in the political arena. Indeed, she is not even a citizen of the state in which the laws that constrained her opportunities were enacted. New York wineries had succeeded in gaining exemptions from the onerous direct-shipment laws for themselves, but outsiders like Juanita Swedenburg—even banded together in a trade association and aligned with New York consumers who wanted to purchase their wines—were no match in the legislative arena against the powerful liquor-distributor oligopoly and its lobbyists and political contributions.

So the only recourse for Juanita Swedenburg was through the courts, wielding the commerce clause, which was made part of the Constitution precisely to protect the ability of people like her to engage in commerce throughout the nation. In the judicial arena, despite the resources arrayed against her, that proud Virginia farmer was able to prevail.

But many on both sides of the political spectrum—as reflected in the divergent judicial opinions on the direct-shipping issue in the lower courts and the Supreme Court—would argue that the courts should have deferred to the states and that the result constitutes raw judicial activism. Some conservatives would go even further and assert that courts have no business invalidating laws in the first place—that the entire enterprise of "judicial review" of laws is constitutionally illegitimate.[20]

As I will discuss in the following pages, federal courts have overstepped their constitutional bounds in many instances over the past two centuries. Judicial activism in many instances is inappropriate and presents a serious challenge to the rule of law.

But in our efforts to curb improper judicial activism, we should be very wary about throwing out the baby with the bath water. For better or worse, courts in a free society are the ultimate guardians of our most precious liberties. As Justice Ginsburg recently observed, courts provide a vital safeguard "against oppressive government and stirred-up majorities."[21] Alone among the branches of government, the judiciary is charged with the vital responsibility of standing up for the rights of the individual against the government leviathan, no matter how broad the democratic mandate.

Were it otherwise, were we to indulge the recurrent impulse to curb the power of the judiciary to protect individual liberties, relying entirely instead on the willingness of elected and appointed government officials to restrain themselves in the exercise of their powers, the result for Juanita Swedenburg—indeed, for all of us—would be that the rights we hold dear under the Constitution would not be worth the paper on which they're written.

With a proper understanding of the limited yet essential role of the judiciary in a free society, we shall see that the judicial intervention reflected in cases such as Mrs. Swedenburg's is worthy of a hearty toast over a fine glass of wine.

2. Judicial Activism: Everybody's Favorite Bogeyman

Our nation's capital always has been a partisan place, but never more so than today. Republicans and Democrats stridently vie for power apparently as little more than an end in itself. Special-interest groups across the political spectrum engage in vicious battle with the sole operational principle that the ends justify the means. Partisan and ideological rancor makes accomplishing anything difficult—which is often a good thing, considering the sorts of things that Washington, D.C., produces. Nonetheless, the infighting makes for a particularly nasty environment.

And yet, many Republicans and Democrats, conservatives and liberals, no matter how far apart they are on other issues, converge on one premise: that judicial activism is rampant and threatens to wreck our country. Although attacks on judicial activism date back nearly 200 years, what is unprecedented is the shared sense of outrage across the ideological spectrum. "What makes the current wave of judge-bashing unusual," remarks George Washington University law professor Jeffrey Rosen, "is that virulently personal attacks now come from both sides of the political spectrum."[1]

It really is quite remarkable. In the recent U.S. Supreme Court confirmation battles, judicial activism was the major rallying cry on both sides of the partisan and ideological divides. Indeed, both sides even have written books about the plague of judicial activism and how bad it is for America. You'd think that liberal and conservative critics of judicial activism were about to bury the hatchet and become the best of friends, united against the common foe.

But the consensus dissipates rapidly once the common demon is identified. For conservatives, the recent confirmation battles were about ending *liberal* judicial activism. And for liberals, they were about preventing a *conservative* judicial revolution.

Both sides' arguments contain a kernel of truth. As conservatives argue, courts have indeed strayed beyond legitimate boundaries of judicial power, often with seriously deleterious results. As liberals contend, federal judges appointed during conservative administrations have been more active in striking down legislation than their predecessors.

But both sides' arguments are hopelessly muddled and contradictory, ultimately calling for curbing judicial excesses only when the outcomes are contrary to their own policy desires. As Boston University law professor Randy Barnett observes about charges of judicial activism: "Most people who use the term don't have a coherent definition of it. It typically means judicial opinions with which they disagree."[2]

More troubling, both sets of arguments threaten to eviscerate the vital role that courts play in protecting our free society. As Georgetown University law professor Peter Edelman observes, "judicial activism" has become a "ubiquitous epithet."[3] That development threatens to undermine the critical role that courts must play, and were intended to play, in preserving the delicate balance in our constitutional republic between democracy and liberty. Indeed, with the explosive growth of government at every level and the concomitant erosion of liberty, what we really have to fear from the courts is not too much judicial activism but too little.

The Conservative Assault on Judicial Activism

Far more than liberals (until very recently), conservative scholars have concerned themselves greatly over the proper bounds of judicial power. The Federalist Society, a national organization of conservative and libertarian lawyers and law students, has sponsored hundreds of debates on the subject, and law reviews are filled with them. Such efforts to divine "original intent" and to promote judicial legitimacy are important endeavors. Only when such discussions spill over into the political arena do they lend themselves to partisan demagoguery, which is where we find ourselves today.

For many conservatives, complaints about judicial activism are nothing new. Opposition to the excesses of the Supreme Court under Chief Justice Earl Warren helped catapult Richard Nixon and Ronald Reagan to the presidency. Despite the fact that a majority of federal judges, and seven of nine members of the Supreme Court, have been appointed by Republican presidents, conservative animosity toward the courts has only deepened. As Jonathan Rauch observed in a typically thoughtful commentary, "In recent years, hostility to the federal courts has served as an almost magical unifier of a diverse and sometimes conflicted conservative movement."[4] The bill of particulars is long: among others, a Massachusetts Supreme Judicial Court ruling recognizing same-sex marriage; a federal court ruling striking down a ban on late-term abortion; a decision by the U.S. Court of Appeals for the Ninth Circuit striking down the pledge of allegiance; *Lawrence v. Texas*, invalidating Texas's sodomy law; the refusal of federal courts to overturn the decision of state courts to allow the removal of a feeding tube in the Terri Schiavo case; and, of course, *Roe v. Wade* and other decisions recognizing a right to abortion. Some social conservatives are so incensed that they urge, in the words of the Family Research Council's Tony Perkins, that on occasion "the legislative and executive branch should refuse to acknowledge a judicial decision, just as the judiciary sometimes ignores the legislature."[5]

Conservative reactions to perceived judicial activism take many forms but embrace common themes. A frequent line of attack is that federal judges are elitist philosopher-kings. James Dobson, chairman of the Christian conservative group Focus on the Family, charges that federal judges are "unelected and unaccountable and arrogant and imperious and determined to redesign the culture according to their own biases and values, and they're out of control."[6] For such conservatives, decisions such as *Lawrence* are "raw judicial activism at its worst," in the words of Scott Lively, director of the Pro-Family Law Center.[7]

Indeed, Justice Antonin Scalia himself has condemned such judicial activism in (typically) strong terms. Charging that "the court has taken sides in a culture war," Scalia declared that the Texas sodomy decision "is the product of a court, which is the product of a law-profession culture, that has largely signed on to the so-called homosexual agenda, by which I mean the agenda promoted by some homosexual activists directed at eliminating the moral opprobrium that has traditionally attached to homosexual conduct."[8]

Likewise, President George W. Bush condemned "activist judges" who "have begun redefining marriage by court order, without regard for the will of the people and their elected representatives."[9] His response to the Massachusetts state court ruling allowing gay marriages was to endorse a federal constitutional amendment to outlaw them—a curious position for a self-professed champion of state autonomy, given that it would federalize an activity (marriage) traditionally left to state discretion.

Other conservatives condemn judicial intrusions into executive power—at least while Republicans are in control of the executive branch. As a parting salvo when he resigned as attorney general, John Ashcroft condemned "excessive judicial encroachment on functions assigned to the president," such as second-guessing the war on terrorism. "Ideologically driven courts have disregarded and dismissed the president's evaluations of foreign-policy concerns in favor of theories generated by academic elites, foreign bodies and judicial imagination."[10]

Concerns about judicial activism permeate the legislative arena as well. Sen. John Cornyn (R-TX) suggested that "there may be some connection between the perception in some quarters . . . where judges are making political decisions yet are unaccountable to the public, that it builds and builds to the point where some people engage in violence, certainly without any justification."[11] At the conference "Confronting the Judicial War on Faith," Michael Schwartz, chief of staff to Sen. Tom Coburn (R-OK), urged that "mass impeachment" of federal judges might be necessary. Former House majority leader Tom DeLay (R-TX) charged that "the judiciary branch of our government has overstepped its authority on countless occasions, overturning and in some cases just ignoring the legitimate will of the people," and he proclaimed congressional authority to "set the parameters" of court jurisdiction as one possible response.[12] Numerous proposals have surfaced to do just that.[13] Indeed, in what the *San Francisco Chronicle* termed an "unprecedented incursion into judicial terrain," the House of Representatives voted in July 2004 to strip federal courts of jurisdiction over the 1996 Defense of Marriage Act.[14] And, of course, Congress voted to create federal court jurisdiction to intervene in the Terri Schiavo case.

The most outspoken, and perhaps radical, critic of liberal judicial activism is former judge Robert Bork. He has characterized federal courts, and particularly the Supreme Court, as "the enemy of traditional culture" in areas of "speech, religion, abortion, sexuality, welfare, public education and much else." Bork charges, "It is not too much to say that the suffocating vulgarity of popular culture is in large measure the work of the court.'"[15] Bork has proposed amending the Constitution to subject any court decision to legislative revision and has remarked that ending judicial review of laws altogether would be "better than our present situation."[16] Bork's chilling prescription, which would allow all government action to stand no matter how tyrannical, is the unspoken yet logical extension of many conservative critiques about judicial activism.

The most comprehensive recent conservative critique of judicial activism is a book by Mark Levin, *Men in Black: How the Supreme Court Is Destroying America*. Levin is a friend who, like me, has toiled in the trenches of public interest litigation, and the title of his book suggests aptly that Levin does not mince words. His words contain much truth—but also hopeless internal inconsistency that exemplifies the confused position that many conservatives take toward the judiciary.

Levin summarizes his case as follows:

> Were our forefathers to view the American federal government of the twenty-first century, I believe they'd be appalled. Activist judges have taken over school systems, prisons, private-sector hiring and firing practices, and farm-quotas; they have ordered local governments to raise property taxes and states to grant benefits to illegal immigrants; they have expelled God, prayer, and the Ten Commandments from the public square; and they've protected virtual child pornography, racial discrimination in law school admissions, flag burning, the seizure of private property without just compensation, and partial-birth abortion. They've announced that morality alone is an insufficient basis for legislation. Courts now second-guess the commander-in-chief in time of war and confer due process rights on enemy combatants. They intervene in the electoral process.[17]

Not surprisingly, the list goes on. It is interesting, and a good example of the tunnel vision that impairs many conservatives when they talk about the courts, that when Levin posits the reaction of the Framers to the current government were they to reawaken today, he focuses on their shocked reaction to the growth of judicial power rather than to the breathtaking expansion of federal executive and legislative power. Indeed, were they to glimpse the latter, the Framers likely would have been pleased with their own foresight in

23

creating an independent judiciary that at least would attempt, however feebly, to check the accretion of power by the other branches.

Much about which Levin complains does indeed amount to improper judicial activism, as I will explore in due course. But much does not. What is most frustrating about Levin's (and many other conservatives') complaints is that they are ill-defined and inconsistent. Levin urges the truism that "judicial decisions should not be based on the personal beliefs and policy preferences of a particular judge."[18] Presumably, such decisions also should not turn upon the personal beliefs and policy preferences of Mark Levin or anyone else—but no other line of demarcation is offered.

Levin comes close to Bork's absolutist position without expressly embracing it. He asks, from where does the power of the Supreme Court to review acts of Congress derive? "The answer," Levin replies, "is that the Supreme Court has simply taken such power for itself,"[19] starting with the 1803 decision in *Marbury v. Madison*. In Levin's view, no such power exists. "In the final analysis," Levin asserts, "if the framers had wanted to empower a judiciary with a legislative veto, they could have done so. They did not."[20]

From that premise, then, Levin can consistently argue that any time a federal court strikes down a federal or state law, it engages in judicial activism—and his laundry list of judicial sins, such as banning the Ten Commandments, taking over school and prison systems, and interfering with the commander in chief's discretion, all would fit that bill. Commendably in terms of philosophical consistency, Levin assails the decision in *Bush v. Gore*, in which the U.S. Supreme Court set aside a state supreme court's interpretation of state election law, concluding that "the best decision would have been no decision."[21] To curb judicial activism, Levin suggests limited, albeit renewable, judicial terms and (like Bork) a legislative veto over court decisions[22]—in effect, a repeal of both life tenure and effective judicial review.

The trouble is that much of what Levin decries as judicial activism constitutes instances in which the courts have *failed* to strike down laws. He cites as examples of judicial activism the Supreme Court's decisions in *Plessy v. Ferguson* and *Korematsu*—cases in which the Court *upheld* separate but equal laws and the president's wartime power to incarcerate Japanese citizens. I agree, emphatically, that both cases were wrongly decided and are prime examples of judicial activism. But if no legitimate power of judicial review exists, as Levin argues, from where would the courts have derived authority to strike the government actions down? Apparently, in Levin's view, federal courts always should defer to states and to the commander in chief, except when they shouldn't.

Another example of fundamental inconsistency is Levin's query: "Have you ever wondered how a federal government that is supposed to have limited power can now involve itself in essentially any aspect of our society? The answer comes down to two words: commerce clause."[23] Levin is absolutely right that Congress has dramatically overstepped the bounds of its limited power by recourse to the commerce clause. But how can the courts legitimately step in, given Levin's premise that such review is impermissible? And if Levin's legislative veto proposal were adopted, of what use would judicial review be? If a court struck down a law, Congress could override the decision merely by enacting the law again. Levin's prescription amounts to unbounded executive and legislative power—or, to adapt the phrase of former majority leader DeLay, democracy run amok.

Nor can the doctrine of original constitutional intent come to Levin's aid. For instance, how can a constitutional command that Congress shall make no law regulating freedom of speech lead anywhere other than striking down laws banning flag desecration, which Levin decries? And although the plain language of the Fourteenth Amendment's equal protection clause would suggest that government racial discrimination (including racial preferences) is impermissible, attribution of such original intent to the amendment's framers is difficult, considering that segregation was the law of the land.

In the end, Levin's critique of judicial activism is hopelessly subjective—and dangerous, because it subjects the entire judicial enterprise to claims of illegitimacy. But the conservative campaign against judicial activism seems to be having an effect. From 2001 to 2005, the proportion of Americans expressing a favorable opinion about the U.S. Supreme Court declined from 68 to 57 percent. Among conservative Republicans, approval dropped from 78 to 59 percent and among evangelical Protestants, from 73 to 51 percent.[24] Fortunately, respondents still rated the federal judiciary significantly higher than its sister branches of government.

The conservative backlash over judicial activism also leads to incoherent public policy. Berkeley law professor John Yoo, an alumnus of the Bush Justice Department and a staunch supporter of executive wartime authority, charges that in the erosion of federalism often attributed to the courts, "observers have missed the real culprit": "the Bush administration." Yoo notes that when Bush became president, he pledged to "make respect for federalism a priority for this administration," affirming the founders' belief that "our freedom is best preserved when power is dispersed."[25]

Yet in case after case, the Bush administration has sacrificed federalism to what it appears to believe are higher-order policy goals. It opposed California's legalization of medicinal marijuana. It challenged Oregon's right-to-die statute. It supported congressional efforts to intervene in a traditional area of state law in order to block the death of Terri Schiavo. It proposed a constitutional amendment to override Massachusetts's judgment on gay marriage. It imposed a federal law that displaces state autonomy over education. As Yoo laments: "The best of intentions may be behind these measures, but they follow a dangerous constitutional strategy. Demanding rigid, one-size-fits-all nationwide rules counteracts the benefits of federalism, which calls for decentralized governance."[26]

It is beyond ironic for an administration that came to power as a result of unprecedented federal judicial intervention to decry judicial activism, and it does violence to important principles such as federalism when conservative critics bash the judiciary for partisan gain but invoke it when it serves their ends. Such situational judicial activism does not provide a satisfying standard for American jurisprudence. And it inflicts upon the courts a partisanship that threatens to erode the integrity of the judiciary that is essential for a nation grounded in the rule of law.

But as we shall see, conservatives like Robert Bork and Mark Levin have plenty of company in their ill-conceived judicial bashing—on the left.

Liberal Advocates of Judicial Abdication

The cover of the *New York Times Magazine* was dark and foreboding, depicting the U.S. Constitution frozen in ice, but the caption was even more ominous: "Imagine that the interpretation of the Constitution was frozen in 1937. Imagine a country in which Social

Security, job-safety laws and environmental protections were unconstitutional. Imagine judges longing for that. Imagine one of them as the next Supreme Court nominee."[27]

Did I accuse some conservatives of hyperbole in their campaign against judicial activism a few pages back? Much of the liberal campaign to counter the perceived conservative judicial revolution defines that term. Generally thoughtful liberal academics such as Jeffrey Rosen and University of Chicago law professor Cass Sunstein have written extensively about the topic, and their arguments engage many equally thoughtful academics on the right. But in the hands of special-interest groups seeking to defeat judicial nominees at any cost—and, apparently, in the hands of the headline writers at the *New York Times*—hyperbole trumps reason, and an important conversation about the proper role of the judiciary in a free society is distorted and stifled.[28]

Putting aside the most extreme rhetoric, what is the liberal case against "conservative" judicial activism? Essentially, the premises are twofold. First is the premise that conservative courts since the Reagan administration have struck down more laws than their predecessors. Professor Sunstein has suggested, "Let's define judicial activism neutrally, as invalidation of government action."[29] That definition of judicial activism—where courts are activist if they invalidate actions of the other two branches—is superficially appealing because it is simple, straightforward, and measurable. The second premise dovetails with the first (and was the theme of the *New York Times Magazine* article by Professor Rosen): that a cadre of conservative and libertarian legal scholars and activists (including me), promoting a so-called Constitution in exile, are out to "turn back the clock" on certain constitutional liberties and resurrect others. Federal judges appointed by conservative presidents, so this premise goes, increasingly are susceptible to the cabal's sinister influence.

In this chapter I examine primarily the first premise, relating to the "activism" of the Reagan and post-Reagan-era courts. In the remainder of the book I make an argument about the proper role of the judiciary in a free society, then leave the reader to determine whether that role is indeed radical or sinister and whether the courts have been exceedingly activist or perhaps insufficiently so.

The argument that the Rehnquist Court was activist is made by a number of scholars. Paul Gewirtz and Chad Golder found that between 1994, when the Rehnquist Court assumed its final composition, and 2005, when Rehnquist died and Justice Sandra Day O'Connor announced her resignation, the Court upheld or struck down 64 congressional provisions. All five of the conservative-leaning justices, they found, were more likely to strike down legislation than their liberal counterparts. Justice Clarence Thomas voted 65.63 percent of the time to invalidate the laws, followed by Anthony Kennedy in 64.06 percent of the cases and Antonin Scalia 56.25 percent of the time. By contrast, the two Clinton appointees voted to hold the statutes unconstitutional much less frequently: Justice Ruth Bader Ginsburg did so in only 39.06 percent of the cases and Justice Stephen Breyer in 28.13 percent of the cases. Gewirtz and Golder assert that "a marked pattern of invalidating Congressional laws certainly seems like one reasonable definition of judicial activism," which indeed it does.

But Gewirtz and Golder hasten to add that "to say that a justice is activist under this definition is not itself negative" because "striking down Congressional legislation is sometimes justified."[30] Indeed it is. The obvious explanation for the increase in the number of federal laws struck down, which somehow completely escapes the liberal critics, is not some newfound activism on the part of conservative judges but the remarkable and breathtaking expansion of the power of the federal government. If the federal government constantly presses the boundaries of its power, by definition a justice hewing to the Constitution will find more occasions to strike down laws. In other words, the problem is not judicial activism, but congressional and executive activism. When the political branches exceed their constitutional boundaries, it is the obligation of the judiciary to rein them in. Given the explosive expansion of government power, what is remarkable and lamentable is not how many abuses of executive and congressional power have been struck down but how few.

If one were to conduct even a cursory comparison of congressional history in the late 19th and 20th centuries, the most striking difference that would appear is the presence or absence of concern over whether Congress possessed the requisite power to enact the statute under consideration. In the 19th century, such concerns were consuming. No Fourteenth Amendment would exist, for example, if Congress had not doubted its own authority to enact civil rights legislation restricting state action. By contrast, the contemporary

Congress spends precious little time pondering its authority to do anything.

The proliferation of federal statutes has been astounding as reflected by the number of pages in the United States Code, which sets forth all federal laws. From ratification of the Constitution in 1789, it took 169 years—until 1958, two decades after the New Deal was codified into law—for the U.S. Code to reach 11,472 pages. It took only 42 more years, to 2000, to increase that number by more than 400 percent, to 46,504 pages.

The growth of executive power is even more astounding. Its growth is fueled by a particularly pernicious abdication of judicial power. In *Chevron U.S.A., Inc. v. Natural Resources Defense Council, Inc.*, the Supreme Court in 1984 largely gutted the "nondelegation doctrine," which embodied the simple yet vital principle that the legislative power must be exercised by the legislature and that any delegation of such power must be accompanied by clear instructions of how it should be exercised.[31] Instead, *Chevron* ratified the creation of a vast fourth branch of government: executive agencies, exercising sweeping and often poorly defined legislative powers, unaccountable to the electorate, and uniquely susceptible to insidious special-interest pressures. Indeed, given the narrow subject matter that most such agencies address, the benefits doled out to regulated entities provide an even greater incentive for them to manipulate government powers to their own ends. At the same time, the interest of a typical voter in specific regulations usually is fleeting at best. That combination—concentrated benefits and dispersed costs—is why Madison and other Founders were so concerned about the dangers of unlimited government power.

The *Chevron* decision was couched in terms of judicial restraint. If Congress has created a statute that leaves ambiguities, the Court ruled, the agency's "legislative regulations are given controlling weight unless they are arbitrary, capricious, or manifestly contrary to the statute," and "a court may not substitute its own construction of a statutory provision for a reasonable interpretation made by an administrator of an agency."[32] Although "agencies are not directly accountable to the people," the Court reasoned, "the Chief Executive is, and it is entirely appropriate for this political branch of the Government to make such policy choices—resolving the competing interests which Congress itself either inadvertently did not resolve, or intentionally left to be resolved by the agency charged with the administration of the statute in light of everyday realities."[33]

An alternative exists to "the principle of deference to administrative interpretations"[34] that the Court has embraced: the Court could and should have negated the delegation and demanded that Congress exercise its legislative powers. Failing that, at least the Court's scrutiny of administrative powers ought to be greater, not more deferential, than its scrutiny of ordinary executive or legislative actions because ordinary democratic processes—themselves no assurance that precious liberties will be protected—do not directly constrain administrative agencies. Instead, as a result of the judiciary's abrogation of its duties in accordance with the *Chevron* doctrine, difficult or unpopular decisions can be delegated by Congress and the president to unelected bureaucrats.

Predictably, the growth of government by federal bureaucracy has been explosive, as reflected by the number of pages in the *Code of Federal Regulations*: in 1960, all federal regulations were compiled in 22,102 pages; today they total 146,172 pages—a whopping increase of more than 660 percent in the size of federal regulations in only 45 years. By any conceivable measure, the increase in the number of judicial decisions striking down federal laws or regulations over those same years pales in comparison with the growth of national government power. In the tenuous balance of power between mechanisms intended to control the growth of government and the natural and voracious impulse of government to expand, clearly the latter is winning. And it is doing so because the judiciary too often has chosen to stand on the sidelines.

Ultimately, then, the chief liberal complaint about judicial activism doesn't hold up. Indeed, like the conservatives' lament, liberal criticisms of judicial activism are inherently subjective. After all, a defining characteristic of modern liberalism is to favor big and powerful government; therefore, judicial decisions striking down government power usually will evoke policy objections from liberals. Hence comes the modern liberal refrain in favor of judicial restraint.

Yet where were those liberal adherents of judicial restraint during the Warren era? Would modern liberals object to such decisions as *Miranda*, *Brown*, or *Roe*? After all, those rulings struck down duly enacted laws and therefore were activist. Or is the liberal complaint limited to judicial activism in a more conservative era? Like the critics on the right, liberal opponents of judicial activism fail to articulate any consistent and objective criteria by which judicial action might be judged.

On the left, Justice Stephen Breyer, who apparently has voted to strike down federal laws less frequently than any other Rehnquist Court justice, is celebrated as a paragon of judicial restraint. The thoughtful justice has articulated his judicial philosophy in a recent book, *Active Liberty: Interpreting Our Democratic Constitution.* Breyer argues that "a democratic theme"—active liberty—"resonates throughout the Constitution."[35] Though emphasizing that he is illustrating a theme rather than presenting a general theory of constitutional interpretation, Breyer applies his theory to a number of contexts.

"When I refer to active liberty," Breyer says, "I mean to suggest connections . . . between the people and their government—connections that involve responsibility, participation, and capacity."[36] To vindicate that constitutional theme requires a respect for democracy and, therefore, judicial modesty—"doubt, caution, and prudence,"[37] and judicial restraint—"the need to make room for democratic decision-making."[38] A judge, in this view, should examine a law both in its purposes and in its consequences but should generally uphold it if it was enacted through the exercise of active liberty or lies within the realm of legislative or executive competence. A judge should invalidate a law only if it runs counter to constitutional values, as when the legislation "will defeat the participatory self-government objective itself."[39]

Two problems with Breyer's approach immediately present themselves. First, to the extent that "active liberty" is an important theme in the Constitution, it is overshadowed by a much stronger theme: the rights of individuals and the limitations on the power of government. As we shall see in the next chapter, the Framers of the original Constitution, the Bill of Rights, and the Fourteenth Amendment concerned themselves not with expanding the realm of governmental or democratic action, but with limiting it, presenting to the elected branches specific defined powers while preserving vast realms of individual autonomy. Perhaps that is why Breyer embraced the term "liberty" within his theme. But the liberty he emphasizes is not the immunity from governmental overreaching that the Framers emphasized, but the liberty to participate in democratic processes and to enact laws.

In regard to his purported deference to democratic prerogatives, Breyer sounds more than a little like Robert Bork. And yet, in their respective applications of judicial restraint, Breyer and Bork would produce markedly different outcomes. That difference underscores the second problem with Breyer's approach: its extreme subjectivity. Breyer accuses adherents of original intent with subjectivity, with good cause; but at least such an approach is anchored in the first instance to constitutional text and history rather than to abstract themes.

Breyer's approach, by contrast, lends itself precisely to the sin he finds in judicial activism: judges substituting their own policy judgments for those of the elected branches (or, more troubling, for those of the Framers of the Constitution). Breyer's theory of constitutional interpretation should have made impossible the striking down of school vouchers, given that they are a product of the "active liberty" to which he believes courts should defer (see chapter 9)—yet Breyer voted in dissent to do just that in the landmark 2002 decision in *Zelman v. Simmons-Harris*,[40] upholding the Cleveland school-choice program. After all, the program was enacted through democratic processes. Members of the community were active participants in the process, seeking to take responsibility for the most important activity in their children's lives—their education. And given the appalling condition of the inner-city schools to which the children previously were subjected, an important benefit of school choice would be to increase the ability of the children themselves to participate in democratic processes. Hence all three of the values underlying active liberty—participation, capacity, and responsibility—were clearly and positively implicated by the program that Breyer voted to strike down. So much for judicial modesty!

When Breyer explains himself, he only illustrates the inconsistency of his interpretive exercise. The prohibition against religious exercise, Breyer argues, is designed to avoid "social conflict, potentially created when government becomes involved in religious education."[41] The problems with that view are multiple. First, Breyer overlooks the other part of the religion clause, which guarantees free exercise of religion—which, when combined with the establishment clause, yields an obvious rule of governmental neutrality, not hostility, toward religion. Second, when active liberty is exercised, sometimes social conflict seems necessary, as witnessed in the civil rights revolution in the second half of the 20th century. One would hope that a court would not strike down civil rights laws on the grounds of potential social conflict. Finally, the social conflict is not actual but, in Breyer's words, "potential." When Breyer turns to his examination of the program's actual consequences, he points to the prospect of billions of dollars funneled to religious schools. Of course, that speculation did not describe the Cleveland school-choice program but would in fact describe programs such as the G.I. Bill or Pell Grants, which have resulted in the massive expenditure of public funds by individuals in religiously affiliated schools. Nonetheless, we do not see religious jihads or rioting in the streets in America as a result of either the G.I. Bill or the Cleveland school-choice program, precisely because the funds are expended as a matter of individual choice and because we have a tradition of religious tolerance. None of that mattered to Justice Breyer, for whom judicial modesty can only be said to have given way to personal policy objections to the school-choice program.

Protecting the Legacy

Ultimately, the power of the judiciary clearly is not safe in the hands of the ends-oriented denizens of either the right or the left. In the search for an enduring, objective method of constitutional interpretation that gives full meaning to our organic law, we need to start with the written Constitution and the intent of those who created it. As a constitution that was intended as much to thwart the excesses of democracy as to empower the exercise of democratic processes, a serious attempt to interpret and apply it will, by definition, lead in some instances to unpopular outcomes. But any other method, also by definition, either leads to the emergence of judicial philosopher-kings, who deem their own interpretations of law superior either to those of the Framers or to those of the people, or to judicial abdication and thus to the erosion of precious liberties that in many instances can only be vindicated through judicial action. Thus, we turn now to the Constitution and the intent that animated it to discern the proper demarcation between principled judicial action and judicial lawlessness.

3. The Origins and Importance of Judicial Review

The quarrel of those who question the power of the judiciary to review legislative and executive acts is not only with imperial judges but also with the Framers of the Constitution themselves. Although most on the right who criticize judicial activism urge that the Constitution ought to be interpreted in accord with its original intent, curiously they rarely have recourse to original intent in ascertaining the proper role of the judiciary. If they did, they would find that the Framers intended the judiciary to play a central and vigorous role in protecting liberty. If judicial activism is defined as courts' striking down unconstitutional laws, then in a very real sense, the Framers were the original judicial activists.[1]

Judicial review was not an original creation of the American Constitution. In England, although courts lacked power to overturn acts of Parliament, they often did invalidate acts of the crown and of local governments. Likewise, early American state courts frequently struck down laws under their own state constitutions.[2] Hence the Framers were acutely aware of the important role of the courts in protecting liberty.

The idea of an independent judiciary empowered to strike down laws as unconstitutional emanated from two core principles. First, the Framers believed that the ultimate expression of popular sovereignty was the organic law, the Constitution, to which all governmental actions and democratic processes were subordinate.[3] Second, the Framers recognized that the tendency of the legislative and executive branches to expand their powers was inherent in the nature of republican government. That process sometimes violated the rights of individuals and therefore necessitated such checks as the separation of powers, federalism, and an independent judiciary with the power of judicial review.

The dangers of excessive democracy were keenly understood by James Madison, the principal drafter of the Constitution. In a letter to Thomas Jefferson, Madison warned that the greatest threat to liberty was the people themselves:

> Wherever the real power in a Government lies, there is the danger of oppression. In our Governments the real power lies in the majority of the Community, and the invasion of private rights is chiefly to be apprehended, not from acts of Government contrary to the sense of its constituents, but from acts in which Government is the mere instrument of the major number of its constituents.[4]

Nor should it be presumed, Madison declared, that the will of the majority as expressed through democratic processes was necessarily legitimate. "The prescriptions in favor of liberty ought to be levelled against that quarter where the greatest dangers lie," he argued, namely, "the body of the people, operating by the majority against the minority."[5]

In "The Federalist No. 10," Madison envisioned the rise of the modern state, with special-interest groups (referred to by Madison as "factions") engaged in perpetual battle to redistribute the spoils of government. "By a faction," Madison explained, "I understand a number of citizens, whether amounting to a majority or minority of the whole, who are united and actuated by some common impulse of passion, or of interest, adverse to the rights of other citizens, or to the permanent and aggregate interests of the community."[6] Madison understood that the "latent causes of faction are . . . sown in the nature of man."[7] The only ways to break the power of factions to do mischief, Madison asserted, were either by depriving factions of their liberty to operate or by controlling their effects. Of the first possibility, Madison declared, "it could never be more truly said . . . that it was worse than the disease."[8,*]

Legislatures, Madison postulated, are particularly poorly equipped to resist the evils of faction and to constrain themselves to act within the boundaries of their authority. "No man is allowed to be

---

* One classic example of attempting to control the evils of special-interest groups by destroying their liberty is imposing campaign finance restrictions, which in its many perverse byproducts illustrates Madison's admonition that the cure is worse than the disease. Better to follow Madison's prescription to control the effects of special-interest groups; that is, to limit their ability to manipulate the levers of government to their own advantage. That solution requires a strong judiciary that can strike down laws that benefit narrow interests while violating the rights of others.

a judge in his own cause," Madison observed, "because his interest would certainly bias his judgment, and, not improbably, corrupt his integrity." Likewise:

> a body of men are unfit to be both judges and parties at the same time; yet what are many of the most important acts of legislation, but so many judicial determinations, not indeed concerning the rights of single persons, but concerning the rights of large bodies of citizens? And what are the different classes of legislators but advocates and parties to the causes which they determine?[9]

For instance, explained Madison, laws governing the obligations of debtors could be enacted depending upon the relative legislative strength of debtors and those to whom they owe money. Tariffs and taxes, likewise, could be set in response to the relative political power of competing factions. "Justice ought to hold the balance between them," Madison urged. Yet "it is vain to say that enlightened statesmen will be able to adjust these clashing interests, and render them all subservient to the public good."[10]

The proper course, Madison argued, was that "the majority, having such coexistent passion or interest, must be rendered . . . unable to concert and carry into effect schemes of oppression."[11] One means of constraining that "passion or interest" was to create a national government. Madison recognized that local governments were particularly vulnerable to the power of factions—a phenomenon I have referred to elsewhere as "grassroots tyranny."[12] He warned that there was "more danger of . . . powers being abused by the State Governments than by the Government of the United States."[13] That was because "the smaller the society, the smaller the number of individuals composing a majority, and the smaller the compass within which they are placed, the more easily will they concert and execute their plans of oppression."[14] Madison urged that to "secure the public good and private rights against the dangers of such a faction, and at the same time to preserve the spirit and the form of popular government, is then the great object to which our inquiries are directed."[15]

In *The Federalist*, Madison and Alexander Hamilton sketched a number of constitutional mechanisms to achieve those dual objectives. In "The Federalist No. 78," Hamilton articulated the Framers' vision of the central role of the judiciary in fulfilling the aims of the Constitution. Hamilton viewed the judiciary as the branch of government "least dangerous to the political rights of the Constitution; because it will be least in a capacity to annoy or injure them." Whereas the executive branch holds the power of war and the legislative branch holds the power of the purse, the judiciary, Hamilton observed, "may truly be said to have neither FORCE nor WILL, but merely judgment." Hamilton voiced an important caveat that forms a crucial distinction between proper and improper judicial activism: "liberty can have nothing to fear from the judiciary alone," he remarked, "but would have every thing to fear from its union with either of the other departments." As a consequence, Hamilton warned, the judiciary must remain "truly distinct from both the legislature and the Executive."[16]

Still, Hamilton believed that courts must possess important powers that were necessary to preserve liberty. Hamilton perceived the original Constitution in its entirety and "to every useful Purpose" as "A BILL OF RIGHTS."[17] He explained that "the courts of justice are to be considered as the bulwarks of a limited Constitution against legislative encroachments"[18] and were "designed to be an intermediate body between the people and the legislature, in order . . . to keep the latter within the limits assigned to their authority."[19] Speaking to Madison's concerns about factions, Hamilton declared that courts would guard against "dangerous innovations in the government, and serious oppressions of the minor party in the community."[20]

Hamilton specifically asserted that the Constitution authorized and obliged the courts "to declare all acts contrary to the manifest tenor of the Constitution void. Without this, all the reservations of particular rights or privileges amount to nothing."[21] Hamilton elaborated:

> No legislative act . . . contrary to the Constitution, can be valid. To deny this, would be to affirm, that the deputy is greater than his principal; that the servant is above his master; that the representatives of the people are superior to the people themselves; that men acting by virtue of powers, may do not only what their powers do not authorize, but what they forbid. . . . Nor does this conclusion by any means suppose a superiority of the judicial to the legislative authority. It only supposes that the power of the people is superior to both; and that where the will of the legislature, declared in its statutes, stands in opposition to the will of the people,

> declared in the Constitution, the judges ought to be governed by the latter rather than the former . . . [that is,] by the fundamental laws, rather than by those which are not fundamental.[22]

No better explication exists of the Framers' view of the proper and crucial role of the judiciary in our constitutional republic than the preceding paragraph.

Because the Constitution gave the national government little power to violate rights, the Framers were resistant to the idea of a separate Bill of Rights, which might be viewed as a comprehensive listing of rights beyond whose scope the government would be free to regulate. Others, however, saw the absence of a Bill of Rights as reason to oppose ratification. Eventually the Framers were persuaded, and even here, the role of the judiciary as a guardian of liberty was important. "In the arguments in favor of a declaration of rights," Jefferson wrote to Madison, "one which has great weight with me [is] the legal check which it puts into the hands of the judiciary."[23]

As added insurance, Madison took pains to ensure that the specific rights mentioned in the first eight amendments would not be considered the full panoply of liberties that Americans possessed. To that end, Madison crafted the Ninth Amendment, which provides that the "enumeration of certain rights, shall not be construed to deny or disparage others retained by the People," and the Tenth Amendment, which states, "The powers not delegated to the United States, nor prohibited by it to the States, are reserved to the States respectively, or to the People."

The Ninth Amendment made clear that the Framers believed that the Constitution and Bill of Rights did not provide a comprehensive list of rights; rather, certain "unenumerated rights" that were acknowledged to exist at common law were protected by this catchall provision. As constitutional scholar Randy Barnett explains, "Only a handful of the many rights proposed by state ratification provisions were eventually incorporated into the Bill of Rights. The Ninth Amendment was offered precisely to 'compensate' . . . critics for the absence of an extended list of rights."[24]

Likewise, the Tenth Amendment confirmed that the powers of the federal government were strictly limited to those expressly delegated in the Constitution. The remainder of legitimate government powers reposed in the states or with the people. That allocation of powers reflected the Framers' belief, as articulated by Madison, that "the State Legislatures will jealously and closely watch the operations of [national] government, and will be able to resist with more effect every assumption of power."[25] As Barnett observes, both the Ninth and the Tenth Amendments thus "can be viewed as establishing a general constitutional presumption of individual liberty."[26]

As Hamilton did in "The Federalist No. 78," Madison assumed that the courts would serve as "the guardians of those rights; they will be an impenetrable bulwark against every assumption of power in the legislative or executive; [and] they will be naturally led to resist every encroachment upon rights expressly stipulated for in the constitution by the declaration of rights."[27] In the constitutional framework established in the new republic, then, federal courts would play two essential and complementary roles: protecting individual rights and keeping the national government within the boundaries of its delegated powers. By describing those roles, Madison can be said to be the father not only of the Constitution but also of judicial review.

So, contrary to the ahistorical assertions of some modern-day conservatives, when the U.S. Supreme Court, in the landmark 1803 decision in *Marbury v. Madison*, asserted its power to invalidate acts of the executive or legislative branches contrary to the Constitution, it was not an innovation or aggrandizement of judicial power. Echoing the words of "The Federalist No. 78," Chief Justice John Marshall observed that the "constitution is either a superior, paramount law, unchangeable by ordinary means, or it is on a level with ordinary legislative acts, and like other acts, is alterable when the legislature shall please to alter it." He went on to explain the implications of those divergent principles. "If the former part of the alternative be true, then a legislative act contrary to the constitution is not law: if the latter part be true, then written constitutions are absurd attempts, on the part of the people, to limit a power, in its own nature illimitable." The Court, of course, rejected that view, declaring that "an act of the legislature, repugnant to the constitution, is void" and that "[i]t is emphatically the province and the duty of the judiciary to say what the law is."[28]

In the process of establishing the power of the judiciary to review the constitutionality of the acts of the other two branches, Marshall articulated a principle of constitutional interpretation that is a central facet of the judiciary's intended role. "It cannot be presumed," Marshall declared, "that any clause in the constitution is intended to be without effect; and therefore such a construction is inadmissible, unless the words require it."[29] In other words, just as it would be dangerous and improper for the judiciary to assume executive or legislative powers, as Hamilton warned against in "The Federalist No. 78," so too is it dangerous and improper for the judiciary to ignore or refuse to give meaning to words in the Constitution. For if the judiciary does not enforce the Constitution against acts contrary to it, Marshall observed, it "would be giving to the legislature a practical and real omnipotence," even as the Constitution "professes to restrict [its] powers within narrow limits."[30]

Despite the Framers' best efforts, the Constitution's protections of individual rights and limitations on the power of government proved incomplete. True, states did resist such exercises of national power as the imposition of tariffs, the creation of a national bank, and a national program of public works (not always effectively). But the Framers' assumption that state governments would reliably protect individual liberty turned out to be painfully incorrect, particularly given the states' protection of human slavery, censorship, and other deprivations of liberty. In *Barron v. Mayor and City Council of Baltimore*, the U.S. Supreme Court ruled in 1833 that the Bill of Rights—in that case, the Fifth Amendment's guarantee that the right of property shall not be infringed without due process of law—provided "security against the apprehended encroachments of the general government—not against those of local governments."[31] Hence, absent further constitutional amendment, the federal courts would provide no recourse against state infringements of the Bill of Rights.

That change would come after the Civil War in the form of the Fourteenth Amendment, which protected the privileges or immunities of citizens, equal protection of law, and due process under law against state interference. The framers of the Fourteenth Amendment, like the Framers of the original Constitution, were infused with the principles of natural rights. As legal historian Michael Kent Curtis relates, "perhaps the most common . . . refrain in the Congress was that life, liberty, and property of American citizens must be protected against denial by the states."[32]

The Reconstruction Congress that enacted the Fourteenth Amendment recognized that it was engaged in a radical remaking of national and state powers, designed to create a more effective safeguard for individual rights.[33] As expressed by Rep. William Lawrence, the new protections of individual rights were "scarcely less to the people of this country than Magna Charta was to the people of England."[34] In overturning the *Barron* decision, by necessary implication the Fourteenth Amendment extended power to the federal courts to protect rights against state deprivations, a power expressly conferred by Congress shortly following enactment of the Fourteenth Amendment through section 1983 of title 42 of the *U.S. Code*, which provides a right of action to challenge deprivations of federally protected rights by state officials acting "under color of law."

For those who value freedom, we owe a tremendous debt to the Framers of the original Constitution and the Fourteenth Amendment for providing for judicial review of actions by the national and local governments. That is not to say that we agree with all judicial opinions or that the judiciary has always lived up to its end of the bargain (indeed, emphatically it has not, as I discuss later in this book). Even Madison cautioned that "constitutional meaning will frequently be contested not because some judges are incompetent or because they dishonestly substitute their will for that of the legislature, but because constitutional interpretation requires judgments that are genuinely difficult."[35] But by and large, where courts have struck down as unconstitutional actions of the executive and legislative branches, they have protected freedom when the other branches of government have failed to do so. Indeed, the gravest deprivations of liberty have occurred not when the courts have exercised too much power but when they have exercised too much restraint.

For all those reasons, the concept of "judicial activism," particularly in the pejorative sense in which it is almost always used, is not very descriptive. Sometimes the judiciary has a constitutional duty to be activist, and sometimes it has a duty to refrain from acting. The better term to connote improper judicial activism might be judicial lawlessness: that is, where courts exercise powers assigned to other branches of government or ignore the clear meaning of the Constitution or decide cases by reference to authority other than the Constitution.

The Framers' understanding of the role of the judiciary suggests the boundaries between proper and improper judicial activism.

Although the boundaries are not by their nature always clear, the principles of judicial review inherent in our constitutional framework and discernible from the constitutional meaning can be described as follows:

- The courts should carefully review all contested actions of national, state, and local governments that implicate individual liberty.
- To the extent that courts indulge any presumptions in such cases, they should apply not a presumption of constitutionality, but a presumption of liberty.
- Because the national government by its nature is a government of expressly enumerated powers, in any case that presents a clash between national power and individual liberty or between national and state powers, the courts should search the Constitution to determine whether the asserted power exists and whether it has been exercised in a manner that does not improperly restrict individual liberty. If the asserted power does not exist, its exercise is void.
- The courts should give meaning to every word in the Constitution.
- The courts should exercise only judicial rather than legislative or executive powers.

This understanding of the proper role of the judiciary is at once broad yet circumscribed. While assigning the judiciary a central role in protecting individual liberty as intended by the Framers, it gives wide latitude to democratic processes exercised in proper ways and directed toward proper ends. It obligates government, where its actions diminish liberty, to demonstrate that its exercise of power is directed toward a legitimate governmental objective and is necessary to that task. If this prescription seems radical, it is only because of how far away from a presumption of liberty the pendulum has swung since the founding of our republic, as specific examples in the coming pages will illustrate.

Some would object, in contradiction to the Framers' design, that the fate of democratically produced legislation should not be subjected to the whims of unelected philosopher-kings. It is difficult to conceive how the design could be different and still achieve its intended aims of holding governments to their assigned powers and protecting individual liberty. Were governments left to judge the limits of their own power, given the nature of ordinary humans (much less the nature of ordinary politicians), that power would be without limit. Were courts elected and were judges not invested with lifetime tenure, they would be more political than they already are, again defeating the enterprise of providing a check against democratic excesses. To paraphrase Winston Churchill, the Framers' system of judicial review is the worst possible system, except for all the others.

Nor in any case can we truly be said to live in a democracy reflective of genuine majority will. Voter participation, even in national elections, is miserably low; at the level of city councils and school boards, it is even lower. Most citizens do not know the names of their representatives in Congress, much less their state legislators, county commissioners, city council members, or school board members—even though the further down one goes on the governmental food chain, the greater the effect the officials exert over our lives. Much of government power at every level today is exercised by unelected agencies and authorities that have only the barest democratic accountability. Even when voters take direct action—through initiatives, bond issues, and the like—they often lack basic understanding of what they are voting on. Elections, particularly at the local level, are dominated by special interest groups, and in the legislative arena, those groups are especially powerful. All of these dangers were apprehended by the Framers, and the courts were one of the central mechanisms they created to check the expansion of government power and the erosion of liberty.

At the same time, although federal courts are designed through lifetime tenure of judges to be immune to direct and ordinary democratic pressures, they are still subject to indirect democratic influence. Federal judges are nominated, of course, by the president, and confirmed by the U.S. Senate, which exercises varying degrees of scrutiny pursuant to its role of "advice and consent." Indeed, Jeffrey Rosen argues that the courts are the most democratic branch of government, noting that over the years the Supreme Court generally has reflected majority sentiment.[36] Sometimes, as in *Brown v. Board of Education*, the Court will make a moral judgment that inflames public opinion. But when it strays too far from majority consensus, as in the Warren Court, democratic correctability sets in as courts become a campaign issue and the executive and legislative branches are given a mandate to reshape the judiciary. President Franklin D. Roosevelt reacted to judicial interference with his New Deal policies through his infamous "court-packing" scheme, which did not work politically but succeeded in procuring the intended judicial obeisance. Certainly the role of the courts was no small factor in the election of Richard Nixon. In that regard, the Warren Court is very much the father of the Rehnquist Court. Since then, Republican presidential candidates have promised the appointment of "strict constructionists" to the federal bench, while Democrats have promised to appoint judges who will honor *Roe v. Wade.* The sum is that the executive and legislative branches are far less democratic, and the judicial branch more democratic, than was intended or is generally perceived.

If anything, the federal courts, and particularly some members of the U.S. Supreme Court, are probably too sensitive to public opinion. Courts are supposed to apply neutral principles. That is the essence of the rule of law.

So how does one go about the task of interpreting the Constitution in good faith? Here it is useful to differentiate between two approaches: original intent and textualism. Both are directed toward discerning the original meaning of the Constitution, but they display a subtle yet important difference. Where an adherent of original intent finds constitutional text to be ambiguous, the next step is to discern the intent of the provision's Framers. But that can be a hazardous and subjective enterprise. Which drafters or ratifiers are authoritative? How can we be sure about their intent? What if they subsequently changed their mind (Jefferson and Madison were notorious for that, especially during their presidencies). How can we resolve differences among drafters and ratifiers? Often (as I can attest as an advocate), two equally compelling versions of original intent can be produced by picking and choosing among different drafters and their often varying statements.

By contrast, textualists also start with the plain meaning of the text, but if it is ambiguous, they will consult the structure, purpose, and history of the provision. Structure relates to the internal relationship among provisions of the Constitution and to its overall framework of government. Purpose is discerned from the intent of the drafters or ratifiers, so that intent still plays a part but is contextual rather than dispositive. History involves the law or practices that preceded involvement, as well as early postenactment interpretations.[37] Among the alternate approaches, textualism seems best suited to produce objectively the original meaning of constitutional provisions.

But why go through such a tedious exercise? Why adhere to the doctrine of original meaning as opposed to some other mode of constitutional interpretation? Why not prefer a "living Constitution," whose meaning evolves with the times? Why should we be bound by determinations made over two centuries ago by people who are long dead?

"The principal benefit of a written constitution is that it subjects judges, legislatures, and executive officials to rules and principles that they cannot unilaterally change," explains Prof. Randy Barnett, "even to reach results that these officials (and law professors) consider superior [to] those provided by the text of the written constitution as enacted."[38] Certainly, discerning and applying original meaning is not an exact science. Judges of good will can read the same words and history and come up with different outcomes. When one factors in subjective philosophical values, outcomes among adherents of textualism can vary significantly.

Yet it is difficult to imagine any other process that would produce more consistent results or that would invest the judiciary with the credibility that is essential for it to function effectively. The Constitution was the product of difficult yet broad consensus in the historical context in which it was adopted. It truly is a social compact, more than any statutes, regulations, or judicial decisions ever could represent. If we value the rule of law, no substitute exists for a good-faith effort to apply the meaning of the Constitution.

Though times and circumstances change, the principles embodied in the Constitution were meant to be enduring. Indeed, to permit a departure from those principles because of changing or exigent circumstances has the inevitable effect of eroding the liberties that make ours a free society. That is why such principles as free speech and due process are cast by the Constitution in such absolute terms. If the right is subject to the political passions of the moment, then it is not truly a right. In times of crisis, the role of judges—neutral, independent of political influences, bound by their oath to the Constitution, and obligated to enforce liberties while exercising truly judicial functions only—is especially important.

Recognizing the imperfection of the Constitution, the Framers devised a means—but only one means—to alter the underlying principles: the amendment process. That process is exceedingly difficult precisely because it requires the same broad organic consensus that undergirded the original Constitution. Any alteration of the underlying principles through any other means—whether by judicial, executive, legislative, regulatory, or direct democratic fiat—destroys the rule of law. The opposite of the rule of law is the rule of subjectivity, confusion, and uncertainty, which when combined with the natural inclinations of government adds up to tyranny.

The next few chapters describe numerous cases in which courts either have performed their constitutional functions or have failed to do so; subsequent chapters examine the often profound real-world consequences of both types of cases. The Framers bequeathed us the best system ever devised to protect the freedom and dignity of humankind. It is that rich legacy that we are morally obligated to preserve.

4. Judicial Activism: The Bad and the Good

In moving from the abstract to the concrete, applying the principles outlined in the preceding chapter is useful for examining specific instances in which the courts have strayed beyond appropriate judicial boundaries—as well as instances in which horrible deprivations of liberty would have occurred were it not for judicial intervention. The discussion here of decisions ranging roughly from the 1890s to the 1970s is far from exhaustive but is merely illustrative and thematic. Many more specific instances of both good and bad judicial activism are discussed in subsequent chapters. Ultimately I hope the reader will join me in concluding that the question of the proper role of the judiciary in a free society is tremendously important and that application of a consistent set of principles is necessary both to constrain the judiciary where appropriate and to unleash it where freedom demands.

The Judiciary Loosens Its Constitutional Tethers

Compiling a "greatest hits" of the worst American judicial opinions is difficult. Like reality TV, so much bad material exists from which to choose.[1] But two of the cases are easy to choose, for they obliterated two of the three protections of the then recently enacted Fourteenth Amendment. They illustrate well the point that the worst judicial activism occurs not when the judiciary acts too expansively, but when it fails to act at all. The human consequences of those two instances of judicial activism were grievous and remain with us even today.

In *The Slaughter-House Cases*[2] (which I discuss in greater detail in chapter 7), the U.S. Supreme Court by a 5-4 vote eviscerated the "privileges or immunities" clause of the Fourteenth Amendment, the first of the three provisions of that amendment and the only one that, on its face, protects substantive liberties. The 1873 ruling upheld

a state-imposed slaughterhouse monopoly that destroyed the livelihoods of scores of butchers in Louisiana. The rights of free labor
and freedom of contract, which were among the liberties intended
to be protected as "privileges or immunities," thereby were lost.*

Ironically, the Court's holding in *Slaughter-House* sowed the jurisprudential seeds for the second major judicial abdication, *Plessy v.
Ferguson*. In *Plessy*, a railway patron who was one-eighth black was
arrested for attempting to board a whites-only car in contravention
of Louisiana law. Because *Slaughter-House* had jettisoned the most
obvious and constitutionally grounded liberty that Plessy could have
asserted—freedom of contract—he was forced to invoke the equal
protection clause. That should have been enough, for the command
of the clause is plain. But Plessy had to convince the Court that the
Fourteenth Amendment was intended to set aside the widespread
segregation laws that existed at the time the amendment was
adopted.

The majority in *Plessy* sounds a great deal like both modern conservative and liberal apostles of judicial restraint. "So far, then, as a
conflict with the fourteenth amendment is concerned," the majority
reasoned, "the case reduces itself to the question whether the statute
. . . is a reasonable regulation, and with respect to this there must
necessarily be a large discretion on the part of the legislature." This
"reasonableness" test and the presumption of constitutionality are
hallmarks of judicial deference to the legislative branch championed
by many liberals and conservatives. The majority went on to articulate what remains the modern view of judicial restraint championed
by many conservatives: "In determining the question of reasonableness, [the legislature] is at liberty to act with reference to the established usages, customs, and traditions of the people, and with a
view to the promotion of their comfort, and the preservation of the

---

* *Slaughter-House* marks a clear delineation between self-styled proponents of origi-
nal intent whose real goal is judicial castration and those who recognize that the
Framers intended that the judiciary should give meaning to all commands of the
Constitution. Robert Bork, for instance, says he cannot fathom the meaning of "privileges or immunities"; therefore, the courts should ignore the command altogether.
Hence in his view, *Slaughter-House* was "a narrow victory for judicial moderation."
Robert H. Bork, *The Tempting of America* (New York: Free Press, 1990), pp. 37–39. By
contrast, true proponents of originalism would look first to the meaning of the words
as understood at the time the amendment was crafted, and if they are still ambiguous,
then look to the intent and theory underlying the command.

public peace and good order." Applying that deferential standard, "we cannot say that a law which authorizes or even requires the separation of the two races in public conveyances is unreasonable."[3]

Note the crucial judicial abdication: popular custom expressed through legislative action trumps the Constitution and individual liberty. The Court's failure to enforce the equal protection guarantee (much less the protection of privileges or immunities of citizens) continues to haunt us to this day, and although *Plessy* is universally condemned, its "reasonableness" test and deference to the legislature remain with us outside the context of race.

The sole *Plessy* dissenter, Justice John Harlan, took a different approach more consistent with the proper role of judging. Starting with the clear constitutional command, he declared, "In respect of civil rights, common to all citizens, the constitution of the United States does not . . . permit any public authority to know the race of those entitled to be protected in the enjoyment of such rights."[4] But tacitly acknowledging that the words of the constitutional prohibition were at variance with widespread accepted practice, he sounded the underlying theme that animated the concept of equal protection. "[I]n view of the constitution," Harlan declared, "there is in this country no superior, dominant, ruling class of citizens. There is no caste here. Our constitution is color-blind, and neither knows nor tolerates classes among citizens. In respect of our civil rights, all citizens are equal before the law. The humblest is the peer of the most powerful." Given that central principle, Harlan concluded, "It is therefore to be regretted that this high tribunal, the final expositor of the fundamental law of the land, has reached the conclusion that it is competent for a state to regulate the enjoyment by citizens of their civil rights solely upon the basis of race."[5]

If we could go back in time and undo only a single judicial decision in all of American history, surely most of us would agree *Plessy* would be the one. Yet at the time, it was cheered by a majority of Americans—and certainly by advocates of judicial restraint. Clearly it upheld the social proclivities of the people, expressed through democratic processes. To adopt Justice Harlan's dissent would have been to substitute the judiciary's view of the constitutionality of a law for the view of the people's elected representatives. That, of course, is exactly what should have happened. But it did not—and all of us have suffered the consequences. *Plessy* illustrates in the most graphic way the dangers of judicial *inactivism* in a free society.

Judicial activism in both of its worst forms occurred during the New Deal, as the Supreme Court further constricted its protection of individual rights while abetting a sweeping expansion of the powers of national government.[6] Having dispensed with the privileges or immunities clause in *Slaughter-House* and the equal protection clause in *Plessy*, the Court by a 5-4 vote proceeded to gut the contract clause in a 1934 decision, *Home Building & Loan Association v. Blaisdell*. The Court reviewed a Depression-era state statute that prevented mortgage companies from foreclosing defaulted mortgages for a certain period of time. The Court acknowledged up front that the mortgage contracts were valid. Was it permissible for the state to abrogate its clear terms regarding foreclosure?

The clear language of article I, section 10, of the Constitution suggests not: "No State shall . . . pass any . . . Law impairing the Obligation of Contract." Moreover, the majority decision by Chief Justice Charles Evans Hughes indicated that the Depression had not altered the Constitution. "Emergency does not create power," he declared. "The Constitution was adopted in a period of grave emergency. Its grants of power to the federal government and its limitation of the power of the States were determined in the light of emergency, and they are not altered by emergency."[7]

Furthermore, the contract clause was adopted, the Court noted, precisely to prevent the abrogation of contracts in times of economic crisis. "The widespread distress following the revolutionary period and the plight of debtors had called forth in the States an ignoble array of legislative schemes for the defeat of creditors and the invasion of contractual obligations," Hughes explained. He quoted *The Federalist* and an early opinion by Chief Justice John Marshall to precisely that effect.[8]

But remarkably, the Court then proceeded to ignore the language, historical context, and purpose and to largely read the clause out of the Constitution. Finding that "the prohibition is not absolute and is not to be read with literal exactness like a mathematical formula,"[9] the majority ruled that it was permissible for a state to exercise its police power "in directly preventing the immediate and literal enforcement of contractual obligations by a temporary and conditional restraint, where vital public interests would otherwise suffer."[10] In other words, if the emergency is big enough and the deprivation is small enough, the Court can ignore the language and purpose of an express and unequivocal restraint on state power.

How could the Court accomplish such a feat? In this case, the Court said, through precedent that had narrowed the scope of the contract clause prohibition. "The vast body of law which has developed was unknown to the [founding] fathers," the Court acknowledged, "but it is believed to have preserved the essential content and spirit of the Constitution." It was a plain instance of the Court's adapting the Constitution to changing times. "With a growing recognition of public needs and the relation of individual right to public security, the court has sought to prevent the perversion of the clause through its use as an instrument to throttle the capacity of the states to protect their fundamental interests."[11] The fact that the Founders intended to create precisely such a throttle when states ran roughshod over individual rights was of no moment to the majority. Its superior "recognition of public needs and the relation of individual right to public security" supplanted that of the Framers, expressed through the Constitution, without the necessity of amendment. Though the Court insisted it had retained the spirit of the protection, in the process it had eviscerated the substance.

Justice George Sutherland's dissent moved quickly to the heart of the matter. "A provision of the Constitution . . . does not mean one thing at one time and an entirely different thing at another time," he declared. "If the contract impairment clause, when framed and adopted, meant that the terms of a contract for payment of money could not be altered . . . by a state statute enacted for the relief of hardly pressed debtors . . ., it is but to state the obvious to say that it means the same now." Although the deprivation in the particular case might seem modest, the doctrine would give rise to "future gradual and ever-advancing encroachments upon the sanctity of private and public contracts."[12] The dissenters, of course, were right: the contract clause subsequently has all but disappeared as a constraint on government power.

The Court was not done jettisoning protections of precious individual liberties. In *U.S. v. Carolene Products* in 1938, the Court reversed several decades of judicial scrutiny under the due process clause of economic regulations that diminished the right to pursue legitimate livelihoods.[13] The Court reviewed the constitutionality of the Filled Milk Act of 1923, which prohibited the shipment in interstate commerce of any milk product that was blended with any fat or oil other than milk fat. The resulting products, Congress declared, were "an adulterated article of food, injurious to the public health, and . . . a fraud upon the public."

Of course, the findings were patently false, as we know today given the plethora of products such as margarine and yogurt-based spreads. The law constituted naked economic protectionism, purveyed on behalf of the dairy industry to stave off competition. It did not merely regulate products in order to protect public health or safety but instead prohibited them altogether. The losers in the political process included Carolene Products, which was indicted for selling a product called Milnut, composed of condensed milk and coconut oil.

The Court held that "regulatory legislation affecting ordinary commercial transactions is not to be pronounced unconstitutional unless in the light of the facts made known or generally assumed it is of such a character as to preclude the assumption that it rests upon some rational basis within the knowledge and experience of the legislators."[14] The so-called rational basis test, which today typically requires neither a reason nor a basis, has become the rhetorical touchstone of judicial abdication of the protection of individual liberty.

But the Court did not stop there. In the infamous footnote 4, the Court announced that there "may be a narrower scope for the operation of the presumption of constitutionality when legislation appears on its face to be within a specific prohibition of the Constitution" and that "prejudice against discrete and insular minorities may be a special condition, which tends seriously to curtail the operation of those political processes ordinarily to be relied upon to protect minorities, and which may call for a correspondingly more searching judicial inquiry."[15]

In one fell swoop of judicial activism, the Court created out of whole cloth a hierarchy of constitutional rights, in which some are accorded greater judicial protection while others are sacrificed at the altar of the presumption of constitutionality. Footnote 4 explains why, since the mid-1930s, the most sweeping judicial action negating governmental excesses has involved freedom of speech, religious liberties, the rights of criminal defendants, and the guarantees of equal protection and due process—but not other important rights. It explains why multiple tiers of judicial scrutiny have developed under equal protection, with heightened scrutiny of classifications affecting minorities or women and deferential rational basis review of other classifications. But it does not explain why some explicit guarantees of the Bill of Rights, such as the Second Amendment right to keep and bear arms and the Fifth Amendment's takings clause, have not been applied as vigorously to protect individual rights. Nor does it explain why abortion, which is not expressly protected by the Bill of Rights nor animated by prejudice against discrete or insular minorities, has received judicial protection.

The inconsistent, pick-and-choose jurisprudence that has evolved since *Carolene Products* explains why many liberals of late have embraced the mantle of judicial restraint and *stare decisis* (adherence to precedent). After all, the status quo of most judicial precedents is selectively liberal. *Carolene Products* also explains why many conservatives question the legitimacy of the judicial enterprise in its entirety. Much of the mischief that liberals cheer and conservatives disdain traces back to footnote 4.

The decision rested in part on Congress's affirmative power to "regulate Commerce with foreign Nations, and among the several States, and with the Indian tribes." Again the language is general. As Prof. Randy Barnett has meticulously documented, a survey of original meaning—contemporaneous dictionary definitions, statements made during drafting and ratification, and *The Federalist*—yields the finding that the Framers intended to give Congress narrow powers to create rules that govern the manner by which people may exchange or trade goods from one state to another, to remove obstructions to domestic trade erected by states, and to both regulate and restrict the flow of goods to and from other nations for the purpose of promoting the domestic economy and foreign trade.[16] Any additional powers accruing to Congress by means of the commerce clause are by way of congressional assertion and judicial acquiescence.

Naturally, Congress constantly presses the boundaries of its authority under the commerce clause and other sources of constitutional authority. But unnaturally, the Supreme Court doesn't always push back. Critics of judicial activism routinely complain that when the courts negate a statute, the judges are substituting their political agenda for that of the elected representatives of the people. But the only political agenda a judge should have is enforcing the Constitution, which often requires negating legislation. What is much worse is when the legislature or executive and the courts *share* a political agenda, and the courts become the handmaiden of the other two branches of government in promoting the steady accretion of government power and the concomitant loss of individual liberty. Such was the case during both the New Deal and the Warren era.

For a time, the Supreme Court performed its role as guardian of the Constitution. In *Schechter Poultry Corp. v. United States* in 1935, the Court struck down the National Industrial Recovery Act, which gave to the executive branch sweeping authority to create "codes of fair competition" in various trades and industries. The regulations reached not just interstate commerce, but economic activities that took place before or after such commerce occurred, such as the slaughtering of poultry. Speaking for a unanimous Court, Chief Justice Charles Evan Hughes rejected the notion that the Depression had broadened the scope of government authority. "Extraordinary conditions may call for extraordinary remedies," he declared, but "[e]xtraordinary conditions do not create or enlarge government power."[17]

The Court invalidated the law on two grounds: that Congress had delegated its powers to administrative agencies without sufficient directives to guide their discretion, and that the law exceeded congressional authority under the commerce clause. "The Congress is not permitted to abdicate or to transfer to others the essential legislative functions with which it is . . . vested,"[18] the Court ruled. Moreover, "where the effect of intrastate transactions upon interstate commerce is merely indirect, such transactions remain within the domain of state power," rather than national power under the commerce clause. "If the commerce clause were construed to reach all enterprises and transactions which could be said to have an indirect effect on interstate commerce," the Court warned, "the federal authority would embrace practically all of the activities of the people and the authority of the State over its domestic concerns would exist only by sufferance of the federal government."[19]

The Court's concerns proved prescient: within only a few years, the Court effectively overturned *Schechter* and corrupted the commerce clause to condone exercises of congressional power far removed from the realm of interstate commerce. The new and expanded commerce clause would become the primary constitutional predicate for the modern regulatory welfare state. In 1942, following enormous pressure on the Court to change course and the replacement of numerous justices, the Court in *Wickard v. Filburn* unanimously upheld administrative enforcement of the Agricultural Adjustment Act of 1938. The plaintiff was an Ohio farmer who was penalized for exceeding crop allotments set by the government, even though most of the crop was intended for use by the farmer's family and their farm animals. Congressional authority was not limited to the regulation of actual interstate commerce, the Court ruled, but to any activity that may "affect" it. The Court did not hesitate to postulate such a connection: even if the wheat was never marketed in interstate commerce, the Court reasoned, "it supplies a need of the man who grew it which would otherwise be reflected by purchases in the open market." Therefore, there is "no doubt that Congress may properly have considered that wheat consumed on the farm where grown, if wholly outside the scheme of regulation, would have a substantial effect in defeating and obstructing its purpose to stimulate trade therein at increased prices."[20] Note the majestic sweep of this assertion: by this theory, a person who lives alone and is completely self-sufficient is within the scope of congressional regulatory authority precisely because of his self-sufficiency, not for what he purchases but for what he fails to purchase. If even a hermit affects interstate commerce sufficiently to predicate national power, Congress may permissibly regulate anyone and anything.

As we will see in the next chapter, the Rehnquist Court several decades later began to recognize some limits on congressional power under the commerce clause. Not surprisingly, some members of Congress objected, and the matter became a central focus of the opposition to the confirmation of Chief Justice John Roberts. That movement also is the principal basis for the assertion by liberal advocates of judicial restraint that the "Constitution-in-exile" movement would sweep away the New Deal and Great Society programs. Not at all. Adherents to the notion of a meaningful written Constitution would insist that, at minimum, when Congress invokes its power under the commerce clause, the object of its regulation must have some connection to interstate commerce, or, alternatively, that Congress must identify some other constitutional source for the exercise of its power. The fact that such a modest notion is considered heretical shows how far we have strayed from the rule of law—a journey that could never have taken place without shameful judicial inactivism. The alternative to the modest proposition that the Constitution means what it says is that no real limits restrict congressional power or that courts may ignore the Constitution at will, either of which strikes me as a far more radical proposition. That may be the fervent wish of many, but it certainly was not the intent of the Framers of the Constitution. Given that judges take an oath to uphold, defend, and protect the Constitution—and not the regulatory welfare state—they should have no license to abrogate intended limits on the other branches of government.

The justification of emergency was invoked by the Court two years following *Wickard v. Filburn* to uphold a military order excluding persons of Japanese ancestry from certain geographic areas (which in many instances happened to contain their homes) in the infamous decision in *Korematsu v. United States*. The Court, in terms that foreshadowed the Bush administration's efforts to abate civil liberties in light of the war on terrorism, no longer deemed it necessary even to repeat Chief Justice Hughes's refrain in *Schechter Poultry* that emergency conditions do not loosen the constitutional confines on government power. "Compulsory exclusion of large groups of citizens from their homes, except under circumstances of direst emergency and peril, is inconsistent with our basic governmental institutions," Justice Hugo Black acknowledged in his opinion for the majority. "But when under conditions of modern warfare our shores are threatened by hostile forces, the power to protect it must be commensurate with the threatened danger."[21] Were that true, the Constitution's Framers, fresh from the experience of our land's being occupied by hostile forces, presumably would have thought to have included an emergency exception within its protected liberties, but they did not. That omission was no problem for Justice Black. Instead of searching for an exception to the presumption of liberty, he searched for a specific restraint on government power. "I find nothing in the Constitution which denies to government the power to enforce such a valid military order,"[22] he concluded. The human consequences of the Court's broad reading of the president's (and indeed, his military subordinates') war powers were, of course, horrendous. But as Justice Black rationalized, "hardships are part of war. . . . All citizens alike, both in and out of uniform, feel the impact of war in greater or lesser measure."[23] Some, it seems, more than others.

But the real, enduring casualty of the decision was the rule of law. "[A] judicial construction of the due process clause that will sustain this order is a far more subtle blow to liberty than the promulgation of the order itself," warned Justice Robert Jackson in dissent. "[O]nce a judicial opinion . . . rationalizes the Constitution to show that [it] sanctions such an order, the Court has for all time validated the principle of racial discrimination. . . . The principle then lies about like a loaded weapon ready for the hand of any authority that can bring forward a plausible claim of urgent need."[24] As subsequent history shows, that loaded weapon has been discharged repeatedly since the Court's abdication in *Korematsu*, always with deleterious effect.

Whereas the New Deal Court eviscerated limits on government power, the Warren Court made its contribution to judicial activism largely by means of assuming powers that are assigned to the executive and legislative branches. Routinely, federal courts during the Warren era did not invalidate unconstitutional legislation but rewrote the rules and assumed their execution. Moreover, when Congress passed legislation that reflected the outer boundaries of popular consensus, the Court would expand the laws' meaning far beyond anything that could have been achieved through the legislative process.

Forced busing and racial quotas, two deeply divisive and unpopular innovations of the 1970s, for example, were largely creations of the judiciary. The framers of Title VII, the employment anti-discrimination provisions of the Civil Rights Act of 1964, explicitly disavowed the possibility of racial quotas; yet the courts routinely imposed or approved them.[25] Even though the U.S. Supreme Court forbade racial balancing as the objective in desegregation decrees, lower courts routinely imposed forced busing to achieve racial balance. In *Swann v. Charlotte-Mecklenburg Board of Education*, the Court upheld a judicial decree ordering race-based teacher assignments, racial ratios in student assignments, and forced busing, refusing to disturb the trial court's finding that "in order to live in a pluralistic society each school should have a prescribed ratio of Negro to white students reflecting the proportion for the district as a whole."[26] Federal courts took over the governance of school systems even to the level of minutiae, and judicial control continues today in hundreds of school districts decades after the constitutional violations occurred.[27]

Federal courts also assumed control over the operation of other public entities, such as prisons.[28] In the area of criminal law, in which the Warren Court evoked widespread public antipathy, the Court went beyond a broad reading of constitutional liberties to assume the legislative function of rewriting the rules of criminal procedure in cases such as *Miranda v. Arizona.*[29]

Similarly, in *Goldberg v. Kelly* in 1970, the Court took an entitlement created by Congress—welfare—and transformed it into a right far more robust than actual rights such as economic liberty. "It may be realistic today to regard welfare entitlements as more like 'property' than a gratuity," wrote Justice William Brennan for the majority, given that "[s]ociety today is built around entitlement."[30] Because society had changed, the Constitution's meaning must change as well. The Court proceeded to create "due process" rules that would supersede state determinations that welfare benefits were erroneously or fraudulently obtained.

In dissent, Justice Black took occasion to lecture the Court on the proper sphere of judicial authority. The Constitution, Black wrote, reflected "as nearly as men's collective wisdom could do so as to proclaim to their people and their officials an emphatic command that: 'Thus far and no farther shall you go; and where we neither delegate powers to you, nor prohibit your exercise of them, we the people are left free.'"[31] The Courts were wisely invested with the power to strike down unconstitutional laws, Black observed. But "when federal judges use [their] judicial power for legislative purposes, I think they wander out of their field of vested powers and transgress into the area constitutionally assigned to the Congress and the people."[32] It is "obvious," Justice Black concluded, "that today's result doesn't depend upon the language of the Constitution itself . . ., but solely on the collective judgment of the majority as to what would be a fair and humane procedure in this case."[33]

When the courts during the Warren era strayed beyond the judicial role to assume broad executive and legislative powers, they undermined their own legitimacy in the eyes of the public.[34] Widespread resentment of the courts' excesses during that period helped bring into office Richard Nixon and Ronald Reagan, both of whom preached judicial restraint. And indeed, after a more conservative federal judiciary was created through years of carefully orchestrated judicial appointments, public disquiet over the courts was largely quelled (aside from the occasional anxiety that the Supreme Court would overturn the right to abortions, as well as outrage over lower-court decisions, emanating especially from the notoriously liberal U.S. Court of Appeals for the Ninth Circuit). When courts no longer provided a hospitable forum, liberal advocacy groups that had invited the judicial accretion of legislative and executive powers were forced to find other avenues to achieve their policy objectives. By reining in the judiciary's excesses, the post–Warren era Supreme Court rebuilt its credibility and standing among the public—giving it enough of a storehouse of goodwill to survive rather easily the tumult that followed *Bush v. Gore* after the 2000 presidential election.

Even though judges themselves are constitutionally insulated from direct political influences, a democratic correction mechanism exists for judicial excesses: the people's power to elect presidents and senators who promise to nominate and confirm judges who understand their proper role. Voters who are concerned with either judicial activism or inactivism can (and sometimes do) express themselves at the ballot box. But such efforts take time and are indirect. The best way to keep the judiciary within its boundaries is through judicial self-restraint, which requires deference to legislative and executive prerogatives when the Constitution so demands, but which also requires vigilance in the protection of individual rights.

Good Judicial Activism

Even in the heyday of the New Deal and the Warren era, the Supreme Court often fulfilled its role as the ultimate defender of individual rights in the face of majoritarian tyranny. It protected vigorously some of the liberties set forth in the Bill of Rights, as well as some basic rights that are not expressly protected by the Constitution. Although the reasoning is often muddled or torturous, the Court's decisions in such cases vindicate the Framers' hopes and intentions that the judiciary would invalidate laws that violate liberty.

The Court's activism in defense of liberty began in earnest in the early 20th century. In *Pierce v. Society of Sisters* in 1925, the Court struck down an Oregon initiative, passed at the urging of the Ku Klux Klan, that would have compelled all students to attend public schools. The Court noted that no question was raised concerning the state's power to regulate education, but this law would essentially have outlawed private education altogether.

Nowhere in the Constitution is a right of parents to choose the schools their children attend explicitly stated, nor is the right of private schools to exist. For those who believe that a specific liberty exits only if it is expressly protected in the Constitution, the tendency would be to uphold the law. The Oregon statute was attacked as a deprivation of liberty without due process of law under the Fourteenth Amendment. In a certain sense, however, the liberty was deprived *with* due process of law, because the statute was duly enacted by the electorate. Sounder constitutional bases of attack may have included the privileges or immunities clause of the Fourteenth Amendment; the equal protection clause (given that the statute overtly disadvantaged private schools and their patrons relative to public schools); or the contract clause.

The Court instead recognized a substantive limit to the state's power to interfere with liberty under the due process guarantee: specifically, "the liberty of parents and guardians to direct the upbringing and education of children under their control." The Court applied a rational basis test—"rights guaranteed by the Constitution may not be abridged by legislation which has no reasonable relation to some purpose within the competency of the state"—yet found the statute wanting. Holding that the liberty was one that was retained by the people, the Court declared, "The fundamental theory of liberty upon which all governments in this Union repose excludes any general power of the state to standardize its children by forcing them to accept instruction from public teachers only."[35]

Even though other "substantive due process" cases protecting economic liberty during the same era now are discredited, *Pierce* remains good law today. *Pierce* is a landmark decision because it fulfilled the aim of the Framers to protect "unenumerated" rights and because it protected the fundamental rights of individuals against the abuse of the majority.[36]

At the height of World War II, even as the Court was eviscerating the due process and property rights of Japanese-American citizens not to be ousted from their homes, the Court protected First Amendment rights, particularly freedom of speech. West Virginia, in an outburst of patriotism, made it obligatory for children to salute the flag. The law was challenged by members of the Jehovah's Witness faith whose children were expelled from school because they followed the dictates of their religion and refused to salute the flag. Again, the law reflected the beliefs of the people acting through their elected representatives, but the Court concluded that the law went too far. As the Court in *West Virginia State Board of Education v. Barnette* described the clash: "The State asserts power to condition access to public education on making a prescribed sign and profession and at the same time to coerce attendance by punishing both parent and child. The latter stands on a right of self-determination in matters that touch upon individual opinion and personal attitude."[37]

The decision by Justice Robert Jackson, who dissented so eloquently in *Korematsu*, bears lengthy quotation because it articulates exceptionally well the proper role of the judiciary in such a clash between democratic processes and individual liberty. "National unity as an end which officials may foster by persuasion and example is not in question," he explained. "The problem is whether under our Constitution compulsion as here employed is a permissible means for its achievement."[38]

Justice Jackson declared that the

> very purpose of a Bill of Rights was to withdraw certain subjects from the vicissitudes of political controversy, to place them beyond the reach of majorities and officials and to establish them as legal principles to be applied by the courts. One's rights to life, liberty, and property, to free speech, a free press, freedom of worship and assembly, and other fundamental rights may not be submitted to vote; they depend on the outcome of no elections.[39]

Jackson looked not just to the language of the First Amendment, which is clear enough, but also to the theory underlying the Constitution. "These principles grew in soil which also produced a philosophy that the individual was the center of society, that his liberty was attainable through mere absence of governmental restraints, and that government should be entrusted with few controls and only the mildest supervision over men's affairs."[40]

Jackson recognized the gravity of judicial intervention. "True, the task of translating the majestic generalities of the Bill of Rights, conceived as part of the pattern of liberal government in the eighteenth century, into concrete restraints on officials dealing with the problems of the twentieth century, is one to disturb self-confidence."

But "[w]e cannot, because of modest estimates of our competence in such specialties as public education, withhold the judgment that history authenticates as the function of this Court when liberty is infringed."[41]

Jackson concluded with a ringing declaration of freedom: "If there is any fixed star in our constitutional constellation, it is that no official, high or petty, can prescribe what shall be orthodox in politics, nationalism, religion, or other matters of opinion or force citizens to confess or act their faith therein."[42]

Certainly the most sweeping exercise of what some would consider judicial activism is *Brown v. Board of Education*[43]—the decision that inspired me (and surely countless others) to pursue law as a career. The decision did what advocates of judicial restraint contend a court should never do: it invalidated scores of laws reflecting passionately held social views, it overturned well-established precedent, and it cast America into upheaval. The fact that such an invidious social fabric could have been erected in the first place was the product, of course, of an activist decision, *Plessy v. Ferguson*, which drained the equal protection guarantee of its meaning. It took the Court 58 years to correct its abject error; but in the end, it did so with determination, and history judges it well despite the social strife that the decision engendered.

Some have criticized *Brown* for its reliance on sociological data. Certainly the meaning of a constitutional guarantee cannot depend upon the contemporary state of scientific art, whether hard or social (a defect that the subsequent *Roe v. Wade*[44] decision suffers as well). But the data were used mainly to demonstrate that separate is inherently unequal and that it confers a badge of racial inferiority. The rule of law announced by the Court was plain and straightforward, and true to the core purposes of equal protection: education, the Court ruled, "where the state has undertaken to provide it, is a right which must be made available to all on equal terms."[45] In one fell swoop, the legal underpinnings of legal segregation crumbled, and the greatest injustice in the land was repudiated.

Certainly it is difficult to find anyone who would quarrel with the result in *Brown*. Yet how can it be squared with notions of judicial restraint that value judicial deference to democratic processes and find fault with judicial review? Has the Court—except perhaps in *Roe*—ever uprooted more laws and customs in any other single decision? Again, those who demand judicial restraint on one hand and adherence to original intent on the other cannot easily fall back on the latter, given the pervasiveness of legal segregation at the time the Fourteenth Amendment was adopted. The fact is that if *Brown* was legitimate in striking down the product of widely accepted custom reflected in law, then so are many, many other instances of judicial intervention. Any other approach is hopelessly subjective and outcome-determinative, and subjectivity is cancer to the rule of law.

Far more controversial than *Brown* among modern commentators is *Griswold v. Connecticut,* in which the Court in 1965 struck down a law that criminalized the use of contraceptives by married persons. The Court grounded its decision in the right of privacy. If such a creature as unenumerated rights exists, certainly a right to privacy is encompassed within it. Indeed, as the Court recognized, a number of constitutional provisions, such as the right of individuals to be secure in their persons and property against unreasonable searches and seizures as well as the multiple explicit protections of property, presume a right of privacy.

Unfortunately, in reaching its decision, the Court used language that subjected the entire enterprise of judicial review to ridicule. "[S]pecific guarantees in the Bill of Rights," Justice William O. Douglas declared, "have penumbras, formed by emanations from those guarantees that help give them life and substance."[46] Penumbras, formed by emanations—whatever they are—are not the proper basis for constitutional jurisprudence. They sound more like the constitutional equivalent of gas fumes. Rather, the Constitution protects privacy because government was given power to invade it only under the narrowest of circumstances.

The majority hinted at that understanding when it explained that "[w]e deal with a right of privacy older than the Bill of Rights."[47] In other words, privacy was one of the rights that Americans brought with them, and did not surrender, when the social compact of the Constitution was created. But the Court undercut its own credibility when it casually repeated the error from *Carolene Products* that those rights include only those that the Court has deemed fundamental.

Fortunately, Justice Arthur Goldberg joined in a separate concurring opinion by Chief Justice Earl Warren and Justice Brennan that placed the decision on firmer jurisprudential ground, focusing on the forgotten Ninth Amendment and its protection of unenumerated rights. The rights protected by the Constitution are "not confined to the specific terms of the Bill of Rights," Goldberg argued, and include those recognized "by the language and history of the Ninth Amendment."[48] To hold that "a right so basic and fundamental and so deep-rooted in our society as the right to privacy in marriage may be infringed because that right is not guaranteed in so many words by the first eight amendments to the Constitution is to ignore the Ninth Amendment and to give it no effect whatsoever,"[49] Goldberg declared. Unfortunately the Ninth Amendment was placed back in jurisprudential mothballs following *Griswold*, but the right to privacy appears now beyond question.

In *Stanley v. Georgia* in 1969, the Court protected both the sanctuary of the home and freedom of the mind. The Court has held that obscenity is unprotected by the First Amendment, but in *Stanley* the Court had held that the private possession of obscene materials in the home could not be criminalized. The state properly may criminalize other activities, such as child pornography, and it may forbid or regulate the production of or trafficking in obscenity. "Whatever may be the justifications for other statutes regulating obscenity, we do not think they reach into the privacy of one's home," the Court declared in a decision by Justice Thurgood Marshall. "If the First Amendment means anything, it means that a State has no business telling a man, sitting alone in his own house, what books he may read or what films he may watch. Our whole constitutional heritage rebels at the thought of giving government the power to control men's minds."[50]

Three years later in a markedly different context, the Court in *Wisconsin v. Yoder* invalidated a compulsory attendance law that was applied to punish Amish parents for their failure to send their children to high school. Although the state has an interest in compulsory education, that interest "is not totally free from a balancing process when it impinges on fundamental rights,"[51] the Court declared in an opinion by Chief Justice Warren Burger.[52] While the state's interests in an additional two years of formal schooling were slight, the Court held, the imposition on the family's religious values was not, for "the Wisconsin law affirmatively compels them, under threat of criminal sanction, to perform acts undeniably at odds with fundamental tenets of their religious beliefs."[53] Indeed, "it seems clear that if the State is empowered . . . to 'save' a child from himself or his Amish parents . . ., the State will in large measure influence, if not determine, the religious future of the child."[54]

The Court applied the First Amendment to commercial speech in the 1976 decision in *Virginia Pharmacy*. Here is an instance where constitutional principles were applied to modern times without distorting the underlying principles. The language of the First Amendment's protection of speech is absolute, yet some (including, routinely, a majority of the Supreme Court) contend that it should apply with less rigor to speech involving commercial transactions, such as advertising. In rejecting a protectionist law that punished pharmacists for advertising drug prices, the Court recognized that the First Amendment protects both those who engage in commercial speech and the consumers who receive it. The pharmacists put forward a number of rationales for the restrictions, such as the public interest in preserving small pharmacies and the perception that large pharmacies that charge lower prices do not adequately protect consumers. "There is, of course, an alternative to this highly paternalistic approach," the Court declared in an opinion by Justice Harry Blackmun. "That alternative is to assume that this information is not in itself harmful, and that the best means [to protect consumers] is to open the channels of communication rather than to close them." The choice among those alternative policies, the Court held, "is not ours to make or the Virginia General Assembly's. It is precisely that type of choice, between the dangers of suppressing information, and the dangers of its misuse if it is freely available, that the First Amendment makes for us." The states are free to regulate economic activity for the benefit of consumers (or, alas, to subsidize or protect pharmacists from competition) in other ways, the Court observed. "But it may not do so by keeping the public in ignorance of the entirely lawful terms that competing pharmacists are offering."[55]

The results of the cases described here are a paradigm for proper judicial activism, in which the courts uphold constitutional freedoms against overreaching government powers. In all of these cases, the judiciary substituted its understanding of the Constitution for that of elected officials—but without transgressing the lines of demarcation between the judiciary and the legislature or executive, because the consequence in each case involved striking down unconstitutional enactments without taking on extrajudicial powers. All of the cases involve judicial negation of the popular will expressed through democratic processes—yet all reflect the core judicial role of protecting precious individual liberties that were violated by the people themselves.

Yet for those same reasons, all of the cases violate the rules of judicial restraint that both liberal and conservative critics advocate. Which of those decisions would such critics contend were wrongly decided? And at what cost to individual freedom? Our free society endures only to the extent that the judiciary abides and enforces the constitutional boundaries of permissible government action, and acts vigorously to protect the precious liberties that are every American's birthright. If doing so constitutes judicial activism, it is the kind of judicial activism that we cannot live in freedom without.

5. The Rehnquist Court: A Judicial Counterrevolution Fizzles Out

In the first chapter, I recounted how miserable I was in law school. Three thousand miles from the calming familiarity of my native Garden State, painfully out of place in an extensively planned community that must consider itself the Birkenstock capital of the world, and mired in a law school that despite its extensive racial and ethnic diversity was stultifyingly homogeneous when it came to philosophical diversity, I considered dropping out. Making matters worse was my perception that I was not gaining the skills or experience necessary to pursue my chosen career in constitutional law.

Then I saw something that changed my life forever: a cover story in *Student Lawyer* magazine, the law school organ of the American Bar Association. Depicted on the cover was a man on a horse wearing a white cowboy hat and a black Lone Ranger mask. The caption read, "Capitalist Cowboys: Heroes or Shills?"

I was intrigued.

The article inside described Pacific Legal Foundation (PLF), a conservative, nonprofit public interest law firm that advocated for private property rights, free enterprise, and limited government. It sounded like exactly the type of place I wanted to work. I was overjoyed that it existed. Even better, it was located only 20 miles away in Sacramento. Given Davis's proximity to the Napa Valley, Lake Tahoe, and PLF, all of a sudden the school seemed downright convenient.

PLF was one of the first in a generation of regionally based conservative public interest law firms. For decades, the left had monopolized the field of public interest law. First the American Civil Liberties Union and the NAACP Legal Defense and Education Fund took to the courts, then environmental and consumer groups. The conservative groups were created, upon the recommendation of Lewis Powell (later to become a justice of the U.S. Supreme Court) in a report for the U.S. Chamber of Commerce, to fill the "empty chair" in the courtroom, typically on behalf of taxpayers or business groups.[1]

I ended up clerking for PLF during the summer following my second year of law school and loved it. The organization is strategically creative and steadfastly focused on its mission. But I found PLF slightly too mainstream conservative, so I cast about for a sister organization with a more libertarian bent. I found it in the Denver-based Mountain States Legal Foundation, where I worked for nearly three years after emancipation from law school. The attorneys were a talented bunch, many of whom would go on to posts in the Reagan administration and to other influential positions. To name only two, my colleague Gale Norton went on to become attorney general of Colorado and then U.S. secretary of the interior, and Mountain States Legal Foundation's acting president at the time, Chip Mellor, would go on to become deputy general counsel at the U.S. Department of Energy, president of Pacific Research Institute, and cofounder with me of the Institute for Justice, where he serves as president and general counsel.

Around the same time, huge bursts of creativity and scholarship took place among libertarians and conservatives in law schools, accompanied by the creation in the early 1980s of the Federalist Society. Although the Federalist Society often is demonized by liberal special-interest groups who view affiliation with it with the same jaundiced eye that Joseph McCarthy once cast upon members of the Communist Party, in fact it is a group of lawyers and law students whose members span a broad range of conservative and libertarian perspectives and whose principal weapon in the war of ideas is debate. Indeed, a number of law school deans have confided to me that were there no Federalist Society chapters in their schools, there would be no debate whatsoever.[2]

Coinciding with those developments was a deep commitment within the Reagan administration to remake the federal judiciary. Like the Lincoln administration (which appointed five justices who would support the president's questionable wartime initiatives) and the Franklin D. Roosevelt administration (which wanted to pack the Court with justices who would uphold New Deal legislation), the Reagan administration placed a premium on appointing jurists, particularly to federal appellate courts, who shared its judicial philosophy. The appointments by Reagan and George H. W. Bush of Sandra Day O'Connor, Antonin Scalia, Anthony Kennedy, and Clarence Thomas, coupled with the elevation of William Rehnquist as chief justice, were the main ways in which this agenda was advanced. (The appointment of Justice David Souter clearly was a misstep measured by this standard.)

The increasingly conservative judiciary made the courts less hospitable to liberal public interest law firms (some of which switched their focus to state courts, see chapter 10) and more receptive to the newer conservative groups. The first generation of public interest law firms, with the notable exception of PLF, generally did not fare well: some were largely mercenary fronts for business interests; some were primarily factories for the production of amicus curiae (friend of the court) briefs, which usually have little effect on judicial deliberations; and some were handicapped by political, ad hoc agendas.

The most successful of the groups developed defined, long-range, systematic litigation agendas organized around a limited number of issues. PLF, for instance, concentrated to excellent effect on private property rights, particularly takings. The Center for Individual Rights focused on racial preferences and limitations of congressional power under the commerce clause. The Becket Fund, Alliance Defense Fund, and other groups litigated religious liberty issues. The Institute for Justice focused on economic liberty, school choice, and private property rights (especially eminent domain). It also perfected the strategy of litigating not only in courts of law but also in the court of public opinion, using litigation as a teaching vehicle and enhancing prospects for legal success with powerful, human-centered public relations campaigns.[3]

The confluence of these developments—the emergence of creative and powerful conservative and libertarian legal scholars, the rise and influence of the Federalist Society, the evolution of a strategic conservative and libertarian public interest law movement, and the appointment of principled federal judges who believed in original intent—manifested itself in a significant shift in U.S. Supreme Court jurisprudence from roughly the mid-1980s through the present. It is not an overstatement to say that the Rehnquist Court marked something of a judicial counterrevolution against the excesses of the New Deal and Warren Courts. The Court reclaimed the tradition of grounding many of its decisions in the language and intent of the Constitution. In several areas, such as equal protection, the First Amendment, congressional power under the commerce clause, and private property rights, the Court moved in a decisively pro-freedom direction, in ways consistent with the central role in protecting liberty and limiting the powers of government that the Framers charted for the federal judiciary. But in each of those areas, the counterrevolution lost steam in the waning days of the Rehnquist Court, leaving the Roberts Court either to restore momentum to the search for lost constitutional values or to devolve into ad hoc jurisprudence or worse.

Two points need to be made before proceeding to an examination of the legacy of the Rehnquist Court. First, the "conservative" justices and judges appointed by President Reagan and by Presidents Bush elder and younger were not monolithic in their jurisprudential worldview. Although most adhere at least rhetorically to some understanding of original intent, they follow different paths from that point of origin, leading to frequently divergent results. Second, although the generally pro-freedom track record of the Rehnquist Court was produced more often than not by the so-called conservative bloc—Chief Justice Rehnquist and Justices O'Connor, Scalia, Kennedy, and Thomas—many of the pro-freedom decisions were the product of shifting majorities, with enough liberal and conservative justices aligning to produce positive results in particular cases (often by 5-4 margins). Again, whether such majorities can prevail in the post-Rehnquist era remains to be seen.

On the first point, of divergent jurisprudential philosophies within the overly broad rubrics of "conservative" and "liberal," University of Chicago law professor Cass Sunstein provides a useful categorical framework.[4] Sunstein divides judicial philosophies into four types: "perfectionism," which seeks to make the Constitution the best that it can be; "majoritarianism," which holds that courts should defer to democratic processes unless the Constitution clearly has been violated; "minimalism," which rejects sweeping theories in favor of narrow, case-by-case decisional processes; and "fundamentalism" (which, given that term's pejorative connotation, I would instead call "originalism"), which seeks to interpret the law in light of its authors' intentions. As Jonathan Rauch observes, "When Bush and other conservatives talk about judicial philosophy, they speak with one voice in opposing perfectionism, but they embrace all of the other three philosophies as if they were interchangeable."[5] In fact, the categories are quite different and lead often to decidedly different outcomes.

Among recent and current justices, Scalia and Thomas are original-ists, although Scalia also exhibits strong majoritarian tendencies.[6] Chief Justice Rehnquist was a majoritarian with originalist lean-ings—in other words, a jurist who tended strongly to defer to other branches of government but who often perceived clear constitutional violations by government. Justices O'Connor, Stevens, Souter, and Ginsburg are minimalists. Even though O'Connor had perfectionist inclinations and voted often to strike down government action, she tended to write narrow, nuanced, fact-specific opinions. Justices Kennedy and Breyer, I would argue, are perfectionists, though Ken-nedy leans in an originalist direction while Breyer tends strongly to majoritarianism. Both try to vindicate what they view as the core values of the Constitution, which for Kennedy is liberty (he uses the term in his opinions more than any other justice) in its traditional meaning as freedom from government constraint, whereas for Breyer it is "active liberty," to which I will return later.

As for the newest members of the Court, Chief Justice Roberts seems to straddle the divide between majoritarianism and minimal-ism, while Justice Alito's record as a judge suggests a minimalist approach with strong originalist leanings. Of course, lower-court judges are supposed to be minimalists in the sense that they are bound by Supreme Court precedents. If Roberts and Alito become more expansive in their jurisprudential approaches and Roberts tends toward majoritarianism (as did his predecessor) while Alito moves in an originalist direction (unlike his predecessor), it could mark a net expansion of judicial protection for individual liberties.

On the second point, the Rehnquist Court compiled a fairly good track record with regard to protecting individual liberty and limiting the powers of government to those defined by the Constitution, across a range of issues ranging from freedom of speech to equal protection. In 2000, the Institute for Justice provided an assessment of U.S. Supreme Court decisions between 1992 and 2000 from that perspective.[7] Of 45 cases examined, 35 (78 percent) during that period resulted in a pro-liberty decision. Distressingly, however, over half of the pro-freedom decisions were decided by a 5-4 margin, suggest-ing a precarious balance on the Court in favor of liberty.

The scorecard for individual justices produced in the Institute for Justice report could be skewed in part by the cases the Court selected for review, by the cases the authors selected to examine, or by the authors' subjective biases. But in sum, the report reflects the proclivity of specific justices to invalidate governmental actions—and it generally supports the claims of those liberal scholars who seek to measure "judicial activism" by roughly the same gauge. The report found that different justices were more or less reliable as guardians of liberty depending on the particular rights at stake. In cases raising issues of free speech and association, the report found Justices Scalia, Kennedy, and Thomas most protective of liberty (voting to strike down government restrictions in 79 percent of the cases), followed in order by Justices Souter, Stevens, Ginsburg, and O'Connor; Chief Justice Rehnquist; and Justice Breyer (31 percent). Those results defy conventional ideological characterizations. In cases involving limits on federal government power, the votes were more predictable, with Chief Justice Rehnquist and Justices Scalia, Kennedy, and Thomas striking down federal laws in all cases; Justices Souter and Breyer voting to strike down none; and the remaining justices in between. On property rights, Justices Kennedy and Thomas were supportive in 75 percent of the cases; Chief Justice Rehnquist and Justice Scalia in 67 percent of the cases; and Justices Ginsburg (46 percent) and Stevens (42 percent) in the fewest cases. On racial neutrality, the conservative bloc (Chief Justice Rehnquist and Justices O'Connor, Scalia, Kennedy, and Thomas) voted to invalidate racial preferences in all cases;[8] Justices Stevens and Ginsburg in none. In sum, the justices' records in support of freedom in cases presenting a clash between government power and individual liberty between 1992 and 2000 were as follows:

Thomas	85 percent
Kennedy	82 percent
Scalia	77 percent
O'Connor	71 percent
Rehnquist	67 percent
Souter	41 percent
Stevens	38 percent
Ginsburg	37 percent
Breyer	35 percent

Three of the report's findings may present mild surprises. First, Justices Scalia and Thomas, often characterized by critics as jurisprudential twins, often vote differently in significant cases (see chapter

6). Second, the two Democratic appointees do not display libertarian proclivities, as some of their predecessors did.

But most surprising to some is the propensity of the Rehnquist Court's two "moderates"—Justices O'Connor and Kennedy—to strike down government power and protect individual liberty. Indeed, those two justices often have cast swing votes in cases, but fortunately, they tipped the balance in favor of freedom more often than not. As Prof. Jeffrey Rosen points out, "Although liberals canonized O'Connor as a moderate after she announced her retirement, they forget that she was among the Court's most enthusiastic and activist proponents of striking down both state and federal regulations."[9] Edward Lazarus makes a similar point: "Both justices have shown themselves to be extraordinarily comfortable with the exercise of judicial power," voting to strike down state and federal laws at least 50 times between 1995 and 2000, "whether the issue is unbridled executive branch discretion over enemy combatants, or deciding a presidential election, or nullifying attempts to legislate morality."[10]

Ultimately, whatever counterrevolution the Rehnquist Court set in motion had largely dissipated by the time the chief justice passed away. As Jonathan Rauch suggests: "The Rehnquist Court's most recent years . . . have been a period of consolidation, not adventure. The Court set some outer boundaries on federal power, but within those boundaries, it declared its deference to precedent and to the elected branches."[11] Whether the Roberts Court views its predecessor as having established the baseline for judicial protection of individual liberty—or as having established its outer parameters—will in large measure determine our freedom in this century.

The Rehnquist Court Legacy

In several areas, the Rehnquist Court moved in the direction of limiting government power and protecting individual liberty. Among other positive developments, the Court acted to curb the judicial exercise of executive and legislative powers in some instances, it gave strong protection to such rights as freedom of speech and privacy, it protected private property rights (a topic I will discuss in greater detail in chapter 8), it strengthened equality under law, and it limited congressional power under the commerce clause. In most of those areas, however, the Court began to lose its compass toward the middle of this decade. But a sampling of cases in those areas indicates that the Rehnquist Court as a whole compiled a relatively strong record in fulfilling its role as a watchdog over other branches of government and as a guardian of individual liberties.

In the area of school desegregation, the Court in a series of decisions reined in the sweeping legislative and executive powers that courts had exercised for nearly four decades. In *Board of Education of Oklahoma City Public Schools v. Dowell*, the Court by a 5-3 vote in 1991 held that where the goals of a desegregation decree were largely achieved and local school authorities acted without discriminatory intent in returning to a system of neighborhood schools, the courts should cede authority to local officials. Recognizing that "federal supervision of local school systems was intended as a temporary measure to remedy past discrimination," the majority opinion by Chief Justice Rehnquist declared that local control should be restored.[12] The following year, in a decision for a unanimous Court, Justice Kennedy wrote that lower courts could restore control over school districts incrementally as vestiges of discrimination were eradicated and that school districts did not have a perpetual obligation to maintain racial balance. "Returning schools to the control of local authorities at the earliest practicable date," the Court declared, "is essential to restore their true accountability in our governmental system."[13]

The Court corrected a particularly heinous episode of judicial activism in 1995, when it overturned sweeping judicial orders in the Kansas City desegregation case. The district had been under judicial control since 1977. Court-ordered tax increases funded a series of lavish court-ordered "remedies," such as swimming pools, greenhouses, an art gallery, a screening room, an animation lab, and a planetarium, at a total cost in excess of $1 billion. But the plaintiffs argued that the courts should not relinquish control because student achievement had not improved. The Supreme Court ruled otherwise, holding that the point of extraordinary school desegregation remedies was to ensure equal treatment, not equal outcomes.[14]

The conservative Court, like its liberal predecessors, issued opinions providing strong protection for free speech. A 1989 case, *Texas v. Johnson*, presented one of the particularly tough free-speech questions that test the Court's mettle—and that, fortunately, the Court generally answers correctly. At issue was a Texas statute banning flag desecration. A man who was arrested for burning the American flag during a political demonstration challenged the law's constitutionality. The decision, which occurred during the transition between the Warren and Rehnquist Courts, featured an unusual lineup: Justices Kennedy and Scalia joined liberal justices William Brennan, Thurgood Marshall, and Harry Blackmun in striking down the law; Chief Justice Rehnquist and Justice O'Connor joined the moderate Justice Byron White and liberal John Paul Stevens in voting to uphold the law. Noting that the "government generally has a freer hand in restricting expressive conduct than it has in restricting the written and spoken word," the majority opinion by Justice Brennan held that "[i]t may not, however, proscribe particular conduct *because* it has expressive elements."[15]

The decision exemplifies the vital role of an activist judiciary in a free society. Little question exists that statutes banning flag desecration command strong popular support, but a dividing line between a free society and a totalitarian one is tolerance of diverse and dissenting political viewpoints. No doubt those who support flag desecration bans do so precisely because of the uniquely powerful political message that flag burning conveys. In our nation, the people are deprived of the power to suppress such political speech by the unequivocal command of the First Amendment. "If there is a bedrock principle underlying the First Amendment," the Court ruled, "it is that the government may not prohibit the expression of an idea simply because society finds the idea offensive or disagreeable."[16]

But the Court did not take that principle seriously when it sustained the constitutionality of the McCain-Feingold campaign finance law. That episode illustrates the danger of allowing the elected branches to police themselves with regard to protecting constitutional liberties: President George W. Bush signed the bill into law despite serious concerns over the law's constitutionality, punting the issue to the Court—which promptly fumbled it.

In a long and fractured opinion, the Court upheld an array of campaign finance restrictions.[17] Many of the restrictions were passed to try to cure perverse byproducts of previous campaign finance regulations—but of course, the new restrictions will only lead to new perversions. Traditionally, the Court has held that political speech is at the core of the First Amendment and therefore strict constitutional scrutiny is necessary to protect it. Not so in the area of campaign contributions. Too much money in politics creates the appearance of corruption, the Court says. And that mere appearance has been sufficient for the Court to uphold sweeping restrictions. Ironically, the perceived need for campaign finance regulations itself is in large part the product of the Court's abdication of its responsibility to keep government within the bounds of its powers: so long as government power is so enormous, special-interest groups will connive to exploit it. As Madison predicted in "The Federalist No. 10," both factions and efforts to regulate factions reduce liberty. The Constitution's strategy is to diminish the incentives for factions by restricting the power of government. Until the courts fulfill their intended constitutional role, they will have to confront restrictions on political speech that inhibit democratic participation and do violence to the Constitution.[18]

Although its record on freedom of speech ultimately was mixed, the Rehnquist Court upheld precious "unenumerated" constitutional rights such as freedom of association and privacy. But again, many of the justices seemed to pick and choose which unenumerated rights they would protect. In the case of the Boy Scouts excluding gays from serving as scoutmasters, the conservative justices had no problem siding with freedom of association—a right that Americans cherish but that does not appear in the Constitution—over the angry dissent of liberal justices who promoted state power to forbid such discrimination.[19] But in the Texas sodomy case, when the court considered homosexuals associating intimately with one another, the liberal justices championed their liberty and unenumerated right to privacy, while most of the conservative justices backed the state's power to forbid the activity.[20] A principled basis to uphold one set of rights but not the other is difficult to find, and indeed the arguments in the two cases were eerily similar. Still, seven justices voted to uphold liberty in one or the other but not in both. Fortunately, the Court managed to get both cases right, with Justices O'Connor and Kennedy joining the majority in each.

In *Boy Scouts of America v. Dale* in 2000, a 5-4 majority found that New Jersey's attempt to forbid the Boy Scouts from excluding homosexual scoutmasters interfered with the organization's ability to engage in "expressive activity" under the First Amendment.[21]

That conclusion was curious given that the opinion's author, Chief Justice Rehnquist, usually took a narrow view of protected "expressive activity." Indeed, he engaged in some interesting verbal semantics to shoehorn the Boy Scouts' actions into that category; after all, no one was attempting to suppress the Scouts' expression of their views. It would have been more intellectually coherent for the Court to solidly ground the Scouts' actions in freedom of association, against which the state's interests would be balanced. Indeed, the Court did hint at that when it declared that the "forced inclusion of an unwanted person in a group infringes the group's freedom of expressive association"—but only "if the presence of that person affects in a significant way the group's ability to advocate public or private viewpoints."[22] Perhaps the majority wanted to find a way to justify not protecting other aspects of freedom of association—but in so doing, it left groups like the Boy Scouts vulnerable to intrusive government regulations. At the same time, in disdaining the Boy Scouts' freedom of association, the liberal dissenters undermined their own arguments in other cases that a zone of privacy exists into which the government may not intrude.

And indeed the shoe was very much on the other foot three years later when the Court struck down anti-sodomy laws. In *Lawrence v. Texas*, two men were arrested by police who were investigating a weapon disturbance, but who instead found the men engaged in sexual intercourse in their bedroom. Justice Kennedy, who wrote the sweeping majority opinion striking down the law, was joined by Justices Stevens, Souter, Ginsburg, and Breyer.[23] The Court overturned a 1986 ruling, *Bowers v. Hardwick*, that reached the opposite result and began its analysis with the query of "whether the Federal Constitution confers a fundamental right to engage in sodomy."[24] Revisiting its own query, the *Lawrence* Court concluded that "that statement . . . discloses the Court's own failure to appreciate the extent of the liberty at stake." The real question was whether the government possesses the power to criminalize the proscribed conduct. For the law's sweep has "far-reaching consequences, touching upon the most private human conduct, and in the most private of places, the home."[25] The Court concluded: "Liberty protects the person from unwarranted government intrusions into a dwelling or other private places. In our tradition the State is not omnipresent in the home."[26] The men's actions did not involve violence, coercion, public conduct, or minors; hence it could not be criminalized.

Justice Scalia, joined by Chief Justice Rehnquist and Justice Thomas, dissented vigorously. The Court's decision violated principles of *stare decisis* and inflicted "massive disruption of the current social order."[27] Instead, the dissenters admonished, homosexuals should advance their "agenda through normal democratic means."[28] But the point of the Constitution is that it protects unpopular minorities against government interference. Were the sodomy laws upheld, any logical stopping point is difficult to imagine for preventing the state's intrusion into the sanctity of the home to police and prosecute private, consensual, nonharmful conduct.

The Court also generally strengthened equal protection of the laws in a variety of contexts. But it did so on the basis of constantly shifting majorities depending upon the particular classification at issue. In the following cases, Justice Kennedy alone among the justices voted to invalidate oppressive classifications in every instance.

In *Romer v. Evans*, the Court struck down a Colorado initiative that amended the state constitution to forbid state or local governments from enacting anti-discrimination laws to protect homosexuals. The Court applied the lenient "rational basis" test—but remarkably, it found that the amendment failed to satisfy that test. In an opinion by Justice Kennedy, joined by Justices Stevens, O'Connor, Souter, Ginsburg, and Breyer, the Court observed that the equal protection clause states "a commitment to the law's neutrality where the rights of persons are at stake."[29] Because the amendment placed homosexuals "in a solitary class"[30]—requiring them alone to seek a constitutional amendment if they wanted their rights protected—the government was required to justify the line-drawing. Because the government could not articulate a legitimate goal that justified treating homosexuals distinctively, the Court was left to assume that the real purpose of the law was animus against homosexuals, which is not a permissible basis for governmental action.

Justice Scalia, as usual, did not mince words in his dissenting opinion, which was joined by Chief Justice Rehnquist and Justice Thomas. "The Court has mistaken a Kulturkampf for a fit of spite," he declared, accusing the majority of "tak[ing] sides in the culture wars."[31] But, of course, it did not. Rather, it enforced the belief of the Framers, embodied in the equal protection clause, that government may not draw lines among people with respect to their rights and opportunities without a good reason. The initiative was classic "faction" legislation, where the majority conspires to impose a legal disability upon an unpopular minority—precisely the danger of unchecked majoritarianism that Madison decried in "The Federalist No. 10." *Romer* was one of the few cases involving neither a "fundamental" right nor a "suspect" classification (such as race) in which the Court required the government to justify at all its arbitrary line-drawing. The burden upon the government in such cases of "rational basis" review is not great—but where the review is meaningful, the government often would be unable to meet even such a minimal burden. The judiciary then is put to the choice of striking down laws that exceed legitimate governmental authority or leaving them in place. In *Romer*, the Court made the correct decision to strike down an irrational law that infringed upon individual liberty.

The Court again vindicated the equal protection clause in *United States v. Virginia*, in which the Court by a 7-1 vote (with Justice Scalia dissenting and Justice Thomas recused) invalidated the state's exclusion of women from Virginia Military Institute. To uphold gender classifications, the Court held, the "justification must be genuine, not hypothesized or invented *post hoc* in response to litigation. And it must not rely on overbroad generalizations about the different talents, capabilities, or preferences of males and females."[32] The state established an alternate institution for women, but it lacked the same rigorous military training, owing to the state's belief that women were not suited to such training. "State actors controlling the gates to opportunity," Justice Ginsburg wrote for the majority, "may not exclude qualified individuals based on 'fixed notions concerning the roles and abilities of males and females.'"[33] The Court held in the Virginia Military Institute case that "estimates about what is appropriate for *most women*, no longer justify denying opportunity to women whose talent and capacity place them outside the average description."[34]

The Rehnquist Court also invalidated racial classifications on equal protection grounds, but with a very different mix of justices in the majority. The spectacle of liberal justices voting to strike down classifications drawn upon gender and sexual orientation, but not upon race, is especially curious given that all agree that racial classifications must be subjected to the strictest judicial scrutiny. But Justices Ginsburg and Souter, in particular, somehow have yet to find a racial preference that fails to satisfy that standard.

A majority of the Supreme Court for the first time applied strict scrutiny to a racial preference for minorities in *Wygant v. Jackson Board of Education*,[35] a 1986 decision in which the Court by a 5-4 vote struck down a teacher layoff quota.[36] Three years later, the Court invalidated a 30 percent minority contract set-aside in *City of Richmond v. J.A. Croson Co.*, because it was not narrowly tailored to remedy the city's past discrimination. "The difficulty of overcoming the effects of past discrimination," Justice Scalia declared in his concurring opinion, "is as nothing compared with the difficulty of eradicating from our society the source of those effects, which is the tendency—fatal to a nation such as ours—to classify and judge men and women on the basis of their country of origin or the color of their skin."[37]

In 1995, the Court went a major step further, overturning past precedent to strike down by a 5-4 vote a racial contract preference enacted by Congress. Justice O'Connor, writing for the majority, declared that "all racial classifications . . . must be analyzed by a reviewing Court under strict scrutiny."[38] In a concurring opinion, Justice Scalia urged the Court finally to embrace the dissenting opinion from *Plessy v. Ferguson* a century earlier. "To pursue the concept of racial entitlement—even for the most admirable and benign of purposes—is to reinforce and preserve for future mischief the way of thinking that produced race slavery, race privilege and race hatred," he declared. "In the eyes of government, we are just one race here. It is American."[39]

But instead of taking that ultimate principled step, the Court retreated. In 2003, the Court decided a pair of racial preference cases from the University of Michigan. In *Gratz v. Bollinger*,[40] the Court by a 6-3 vote (with Breyer concurring in the judgment of the five conservative justices) invalidated an undergraduate admissions scheme that automatically awarded to certain minority candidates 20 of the 100 points necessary for admission. But in *Grutter v. Bollinger*, the Court by a 5-4 vote—with Justice O'Connor joining the four liberal justices and authoring the majority opinion—upheld the law school's more sophisticated preference policy. The majority found that the benefits of racial diversity—such as cross-racial understanding and breaking down racial stereotypes—constitute a compelling interest for a government university and that the law school's policies were narrowly tailored to that objective. The law school considered applicants on an individual basis, it did not use a strict quota, and it considered diversity factors other than race and ethnicity, the Court noted. As a result, the law school was justified in leapfrogging certain minority candidates over others who had significantly superior credentials. Justice O'Connor attempted to soothe skeptics. "We expect that 25 years from now, the use of racial preferences will no longer be necessary to further the interest approved today."[41,42]

The notion of using race to achieve a "critical mass" among designated minorities, Justice Kennedy noted in dissent, "is a delusion used by the Law School to mask its attempt to make race an automatic factor in most instances and to achieve numerical goals indistinguishable from quotas."[43] The Court's opinion, as Justice Thomas observed, "grant[s] a 25-year license to violate the Constitution. . . . For the immediate future, however, the majority has placed its *imprimatur* on a practice that can only weaken the principle of equality embodied in our Declaration of Independence and the Equal Protection Clause."[44] The Court came to the brink of finally closing one of the most lamentable chapters of our national history—the classification by government of Americans on the basis of race—and instead tragically opted to perpetuate it.

Another important area in which the Rehnquist Court acted to correct past judicial activism—only to retreat at the last moment—was congressional authority under the commerce clause. As the previous chapter depicted, prior Courts essentially abdicated any meaningful review of such congressional power, even where the nexus with interstate commerce was attenuated.

The Court began to shift toward a more moderate course in its 1995 decision in *United States v. Lopez*, striking down the Gun-Free School Zones Act, in which Congress forbade the possession of firearms within school zones. Although the law's objectives were laudatory, the case raised important questions regarding the nationalization of criminal law, which traditionally has been primarily a state function. Indeed, state officials brought charges against a 12th-grader who brought a gun to school, but they dismissed the charges when federal officials brought charges under the federal law.

The 5-4 majority opinion by Chief Justice Rehnquist noted that the Constitution delegated limited and defined powers to the national government, reserving the remainder of legitimate powers to the states. "This constitutionally mandated division of authority 'was adopted by the Framers to ensure protection of our fundamental liberties,'"[45] Rehnquist wrote. Accordingly, in determining whether a statute is within the scope of delegated congressional power, the Court must ascertain "whether the regulated activity 'substantially affects' interstate commerce."[46] The Court found that the statute "by its terms has nothing to do with 'commerce' or any sort of economic enterprise" and "is not an essential part of a larger regulation of economic activity, in which the regulation could be undercut unless intrastate activity was regulated."[47] Hence the law exceeded the bounds of congressional power. Were the Court to accept the government's justifications seeking to establish a remote connection to interstate commerce, the Court reasoned, "we are hard pressed to posit any activity by an individual that Congress is without power to regulate."[48]

In their concurring opinion, Justices Kennedy and O'Connor addressed the proper role of the judiciary in such cases. "[I]t would be mistaken and mischievous for the political branches to forget that the sworn obligation to preserve and protect the Constitution in maintaining the federal balance is their own in the first and primary instance," they said. But "the absence of structural mechanisms to require those officials to undertake this principled task, and the momentary political convenience often attendant upon their failure to do so, argue against a complete renunciation of the judicial role."[49]

The *Lopez* decision was extremely modest and deferential. Indeed, Justice Thomas urged the Court to go further, declaring that "we must further reconsider our 'substantial effects' test with an eye toward constructing a standard that reflects the text and history of the Commerce Clause without totally rejecting our more recent Commerce Clause jurisprudence."[50] Yet the reaction of the dissenters—and of members of the U.S. Senate speaking on the issue during Chief Justice Roberts's confirmation hearings—was histrionic. In reality, all the Court did was to restore *some* of the limits to congressional power, in essence merely requiring that congressional authority exercised under the commerce clause must actually address commerce. The proposition that congressional authority is unlimited is far more radical and subversive of our constitutional republic than the notion that such power is broad yet bounded.

The Court took a further step in the direction of reining in congressional excesses five years later in *United States v. Morrison*, when the same 5-4 majority invalidated portions of the Violence against Women Act. That 1994 statute allowed a rape victim to sue her alleged perpetrator in federal court, even though each state permitted such suits in its own courts. Though presuming the law's constitutionality, the Court held that Congress could not "regulate noneconomic, violent criminal conduct based solely on that conduct's aggregate effect on interstate commerce."[51] Again, congressional regulation under the commerce clause must be aimed at interstate commerce.

But only five years after *Morrison*, the Court retreated in *Gonzales v. Raich*, in which the Court upheld the application of provisions of federal drug laws to California citizens legally possessing marijuana for medicinal purposes under state law. The outcome underscored Justice Thomas's point in his concurring opinion in *Lopez* that the Supreme Court should articulate a new standard in harmony with the language and purpose of the commerce clause. Because it had not, the Court, by a 6-3 vote (with Justices Kennedy and Scalia joining the liberal justices), too easily upheld a law that was part of a broad federal drug regulatory scheme, despite the law's application to purely intrastate commerce in a state where the people had voted to legalize the conduct.[52] As the majority opinion by Justice Stevens aptly stated, "Our case law firmly establishes Congress' power to regulate purely local activities that are part of an economic 'class of activities' that have a substantial effect on interstate commerce."[53] And the Court took the opportunity to reaffirm the pernicious *Wickard v. Filburn* decision.

The dissenting opinion by Justice O'Connor protested that the *Raich* decision "gives Congress a perverse incentive to legislate broadly pursuant to the Commerce Clause—nestling questionable assertions of its own authority into comprehensive regulatory schemes—rather than with precision."[54] In the wake of *Raich*, the question of whether *Lopez* and *Morrison* remain good law—and even if they do, whether they will have any enduring effect in vindicating the Framers' design of a national government possessed of limited and defined powers—is left to the Roberts Court to determine.

Even though its fervor dissipated in its waning days, the Rehnquist Court was, in the highest and best sense of the term, an activist Court. In many areas, the Rehnquist Court began to reverse decades of judicial abdication, restoring precious constitutional liberties that had been erased from the Constitution and reining in decades of judicial excesses, in which courts had exercised powers that were delegated by the Constitution to the elected branches of government. In each instance the Court struck a blow for freedom—and acted consonantly with the spirit of the Framers.

Yet there was no rioting in the streets, no democratic response. Can it be that Americans like a Court that protects its liberties, acting like a true court of law and not a super-legislature? Indeed, the most serious public reaction against a Supreme Court decision of recent vintage was its failure to strike down the abusive exercise of the eminent domain power by New London, Connecticut (see chapter 8), suggesting that many Americans would like to see a *more* vigorous Court, not less.

But if the Rehnquist Court marked an era of activism, it was a modest one and ultimately spent itself far short of restoring the judiciary's vital role as a reliable guardian of liberty as envisioned by the Framers. It is now left to principled advocates to rekindle that spirit—and to principled judges to keep it burning brightly.

6. Model Justice

Even Justice Clarence Thomas makes mistakes. After all, he voted against me in the only case I've argued in front of him.

But in terms of the art of judging, Justice Thomas comes as close to the ideal envisioned by the Framers of the Constitution as anyone in modern times. As a result, Justice Thomas's jurisprudence merits special attention.

I first encountered Clarence Thomas more than 20 years ago, when I was a young lawyer and he was chairman of the U.S. Equal Employment Opportunity Commission (EEOC). Like many other idealistic young conservative and libertarian lawyers, I was hearing the siren call of the Reagan administration. I finally succumbed when I received a job offer to serve as special assistant to the EEOC's newest commissioner, Rosalie "Ricky" Silberman. I didn't know much about the EEOC, but it dealt with issues I cared about and I liked and respected Ricky.

Shortly after I had quit my job at Mountain States Legal Foundation and sold my house in Denver in anticipation of a move to Washington, D.C., I received a frantic call from Ricky. "Don't worry," she said, "if it doesn't work out here I'll help you get a job somewhere else."

"What?" I asked, thinking she was kidding even as an icy feeling of panic gripped me.

I had written an op-ed attacking the civil rights establishment and calling for a new generation of civil rights leadership. I had submitted it to the *Washington Times*, which had kept it on the shelf for months and unbeknownst to me elected to publish it just as I was ready to take my new job.

Ricky told me she couldn't have an assistant who wrote controversial articles, especially given that she hadn't been confirmed to her post by the Senate yet. Not only that, but among the new generation of civil rights leaders, I hadn't even mentioned the commission's chairman, Clarence Thomas. What a faux pas!

The reason I hadn't mentioned Thomas was because I had never heard of him. In an effort to clean out the bureaucratic disaster left by his predecessor, Eleanor Holmes Norton, and to pursue controversial new policies emphasizing full relief for individual victims of discrimination rather than racial preferences, Thomas had adopted an intentionally low profile. In fact, in the mid-1980s Thomas often was referred to as the "other Clarence," operating in the shadow of Clarence Pendleton, the colorful and highly controversial chairman of the U.S. Civil Rights Commission.

Fortunately, Ricky reconsidered and agreed not to fire me before I started, so long as I promised to stay out of trouble. But at the first commission meeting I attended, I was sheepish about meeting the chairman. When he was introduced to me, though, he astonished me by saying that he loved the op-ed and that he had used one of the lines from it in a speech.

To which I replied, "Don't worry, if anyone asks, I'll tell them I stole it from you."

And that's when I heard it for the first time: the laugh.

No one who has ever heard Clarence Thomas laugh has forgotten it. It is loud, booming, and utterly unforgettable.

I grew to intensely admire Thomas as a mentor and—a true rarity in our nation's capital—as a true statesman. Thomas and I became friends, and ultimately I asked him to be the godfather to my middle son, Todd. I knew both Clarence and his wonderful wife, Virginia, before they knew each other and was delighted when they married. One of our areas of common interest was constitutional philosophy. Both of us were writing about it, and in his case, speaking publicly about it. I found exhilarating his belief that the Constitution was informed by principles of natural rights and that it should be interpreted according to the intent of the Framers.

When Thomas was nominated to the U.S. Supreme Court, Chip Mellor and I were launching the Institute for Justice. The timing was propitious for our fledgling organization, given that we were advancing natural rights–based jurisprudence. Indeed, the early controversy over Thomas's nomination centered on exactly that. The same Senate Judiciary Committee chairman, Joseph Biden, who had ripped Robert Bork several years earlier for taking an unduly restrictive reading of the Constitution's liberties attacked Thomas without a hint of irony for asserting that the rights protected by the Constitution go beyond those expressly enumerated in its text.

Had the battle remained in that terrain, it could have been a wonderful learning experience in civics and constitutional jurisprudence for the American people. But our nation's capital cannot abide such lofty standards of civil discourse. During the Thomas confirmation battle, I learned firsthand how much is at stake in Supreme Court nominations. Ideologically driven groups for whom the operating philosophy is that the ends justify the means will stop at nothing to defeat a nomination—even if it means trying to destroy the nominee on inflammatory yet groundless charges.

A short time before the hearings began, I recall having coffee with Timothy Phelps, the *Newsday* reporter who, along with Nina Totenberg of National Public Radio, broke the Anita Hill story. We talked about the various arguments that the special-interest groups were making against Thomas and about our campaign in support. I was taken aback when Phelps asked me whether I had ever heard any rumors about sexual harassment. Against Clarence Thomas? I thought that was utterly ridiculous. His critics could assail Thomas on his judicial philosophy or his record at the EEOC to whatever effect they could make of it; but if Thomas was unassailable in any realm, it was his personal and professional behavior. What's more, the EEOC is a hypersensitive environment—everyone knows what the rules are and how important it is to abide them. And every employee, from the chairman to the file clerks, knows how easy it is to file a complaint.

Almost everyone who knew both Clarence Thomas and Anita Hill (I did not know her)—whether liberal or conservative—believed Thomas without question. I found that most observers viewed the charges through their own lens of experience. Most people could not possibly know what Thomas's friends know: that he consistently holds himself to uncommonly high standards of personal and professional behavior. Knowing how much his own character and reputation meant to him, the hearings were a painful ordeal to Thomas's friends, even as they were unspeakably wrenching for Thomas and his family.

After they failed to destroy Thomas or his nomination and he took his place as an associate justice, his critics patronizingly began to savage him as a second-rate justice, a lapdog for Justice Scalia and incapable of independent thought. Again, anyone who knows Thomas could safely have predicted that he would emerge as his own man. Refreshingly, the critics attack Thomas for his personal brand of jurisprudence. He has become his critics' worst nightmare: a justice who tries his best to interpret and apply the Constitution as it was intended and not how special-interest groups wish it were written.

As chapter 5 recounts, several recent and current justices interpret the Constitution in ways that are congenial to liberty. However, Justice Thomas exhibits several qualities that make him the type of justice the Framers must have had in mind when they invested the judiciary with its central role in protecting freedom. In almost every constitutional case, he begins by examining not the Court's precedents but the language and intent of the Constitution itself.[1] He recognizes that precedent is important to the rule of law, but ultimately that the Court is bound by the Constitution rather than by its own past decisions. As a result, Thomas is more willing than many of his colleagues to consider overturning precedents and doctrines that are contrary to the Constitution. And recognizing that clarity is essential to the rule of law, he generally eschews subjective line-drawing and balancing tests in favor of unambiguous rules that vindicate constitutional principles and provide clear guidance to lawmakers regarding their powers and to citizens regarding their rights. Finally, he is not one to go along in order to get along: he is happy to dissent from either the majority's ruling or its reasoning rather than to contribute to jurisprudence that does harm to the Constitution.

Thomas's clarity of vision can be glimpsed in almost any of his constitutional opinions. Because he believes that law should be neither mystical nor mysterious, he tries to write in terms that are accessible to ordinary people. Equally important, he applies a consistent interpretational construct, which, if the Court as a whole adopted it, would lead to both greater jurisprudential integrity and predictability. Although I will highlight some of Justice Thomas's opinions on property rights (chapter 8) and school choice (chapter 9), a few cases from other areas of the law illustrate well his approach and style.

An early example is Justice Thomas's opinion concurring in a 1995 decision that struck down an Ohio law imposing fines on anonymous political pamphleteers. For Justice Scalia, who dissented along with Chief Justice Rehnquist, tradition trumped original intent because the Constitution itself is unclear about whether anonymous pamphleteering was protected. "Where the meaning of constitutional text (such as 'the freedom of speech') is unclear," Scalia wrote, "the widespread and long-accepted practices of the American people are the best indication of what fundamental beliefs it was meant to enshrine."[2] Because nearly all states had long since regulated anonymous political pamphlets, Ohio could do so as well.

That was not enough for Justice Thomas. "While, like Justice Scalia, I am loath to overturn almost a century of practice shared by almost all of the States, I believe that the historical evidence from the framing outweighs recent tradition."[3] Nor did he join the reasoning of the majority, which focused on the "value" of anonymous political writing and the works of Voltaire, Mark Twain, and others. "I cannot join the majority's analysis because it deviates from our settled approach to interpreting the Constitution and because it superimposes its modern theories concerning expression upon the constitutional text."[4] Instead, Thomas painstakingly reviewed the historical record as well as the central role that anonymous political tracts played in the founding era, ultimately concluding that the objective evidence demonstrated that the Framers intended to protect the proscribed conduct within the sphere of freedom of speech.

In navigating the treacherous jurisprudential waters of the First Amendment's religion clauses—one of the most muddled areas of contemporary law—Justice Thomas has charted a course in harmony with the amendment's plain language and intent, rejecting the Court's hopelessly subjective, unpredictable, and incoherent line-drawing. One example is a fractured 4-1-4 decision in 2005 that typifies recent jurisprudence under the First Amendment's prohibition of religious establishment clause. Although it couldn't agree on a rationale, the Court upheld the erection of a privately funded monument depicting the Ten Commandments among the 21 historical monuments and 17 monuments surrounding the Texas state capitol. "This case would be easy," Justice Thomas observed in a concurring opinion, "if the Court were willing to abandon the inconsistent guideposts it has adopted for addressing Establishment Clause challenges, and return to the original meaning of the Clause."[5] The Framers' clear understanding of the word "establishment," Thomas found, involved legal coercion. By contrast, "this Court's precedent permits even the slightest public recognition of religion to constitute an establishment of religion."[6] The test applied by the Court—whether the display contains religious symbolism and its ubiquity—"is incapable of consistent application" and replaces the rule of law with "the personal preferences of judges."[7] By returning to governmental coercion as the original touchstone for proscribed conduct under the establishment clause, Thomas urged, the Court would create a consistent rule that in most cases would yield clear results.

Justice Thomas's determination to return to constitutional basics— and the differences in the jurisprudential styles of the supposed twin justices, Thomas and Scalia—are illustrated well by a pair of cases involving unenumerated rights, *Saenz v. Roe* in 1999 and *Troxel v. Granville* a year later. In *Saenz*, a 7-2 majority of the Court (including Justice Scalia) struck down a California law directing that welfare benefits for residents moving from other states would be the same for one year as the benefits those residents had previously received. The Court found the law violated the "right to travel," which was protected by, among other constitutional provisions, the privileges or immunities clause of the Fourteenth Amendment.

The Court's decision was not surprising, but its grounding of the right to travel in the privileges or immunities clause was. As Justice Thomas observed in his dissent, "Unlike the Equal Protection and Due Process Clauses, which have assumed near-talismanic status in modern constitutional law, the Court all but read the Privileges or Immunities Clause out of the Constitution in the *Slaughter-House Cases*," nearly a century and a quarter earlier[8] (see chapter 7). Thomas joined Chief Justice Rehnquist's dissent, which found that the clause and the judicially recognized right to travel were not intended to protect welfare entitlements. But he went on to state that because "the demise of the Privileges or Immunities Clause has contributed in no small part to the current disarray of Fourteenth Amendment jurisprudence"—presumably including the sometimes oxymoronic judicial doctrine of "substantive due process"—Thomas "would be open to reevaluating its meaning in an appropriate case." Instead, the Court exhumed the clause and placed within it a "right" to welfare that the Fourteenth Amendment's framers never intended to protect. The Court's failure to examine original intent, Thomas charged, "raised the specter that the Privileges or Immunities Clause will become yet another convenient tool for inventing new rights" according to the predilections of members of the Court.[9]

In *Troxel*, the Court struck down a Washington law that allowed any person to petition a court for visitation rights with a child, based only upon a judicial conclusion that such visitation was in the child's best interests. The case involved grandparents who petitioned for visitation with their deceased son's children, against the wishes of the boy's mother, who objected to the amount of time sought. An unusual combination of six justices (Chief Justice Rehnquist and Justices O'Connor, Souter, Thomas, Ginsburg, and Breyer) concluded that the law unconstitutionally displaced the parent's primary role in directing the upbringing of her children, as protected by the *Pierce v. Society of Sisters* line of cases.

Dissenting along with Justices Stevens and Kennedy, Justice Scalia issued a Borkian broadside against the concept of judicially protected unenumerated rights. Acknowledging that parental autonomy was within the unalienable rights recognized by the Declaration of Independence and the Ninth Amendment, Scalia argued that "the Constitution's refusal to 'deny or disparage' [such] rights is far removed from affirming any one of them, and even farther removed from authorizing judges to identify what they might be, and to enforce the judges' list against laws duly enacted by the people."[10] Curiously, he failed to acknowledge that in *Saenz* only a year earlier, he had voted to strike down a duly enacted law as a violation of the unenumerated right to travel.

Justice Thomas, concurring in the judgment, noted that none of the parties had contested whether the due process clause protected parental liberty or raised the argument that the right was protected instead by the privileges or immunities clause. Taking as a given, then, that parental liberty is a fundamental right, he found the question before the Court an easy one. "I would apply strict scrutiny to infringements of fundamental rights," Thomas declared. "Here, the State of Washington lacks even a legitimate governmental interest— to say nothing of a compelling one—in second-guessing a fit parent's decision regarding visitation with third parties."[11]

Justice Thomas's adherence to the rule of law is perhaps best illustrated by his opinions concerning congressional authority under the commerce clause (see chapter 4). In *United States v. Lopez*, Thomas joined with the majority in applying the "first principles" of the commerce clause, voting to strike down congressional regulation of guns in school zones. But in a concurring opinion, Thomas expressed his impatience with efforts to reconcile decades of case law with original intent. Examining history, Thomas found that commerce at the time of the founding was understood to encompass selling, buying, bartering, and transporting goods that were exchanged in those manners—and did not include such activities as manufacturing or agriculture. Not only did Congress (with the Court's duplicity) greatly expand that definition to encompass all economic activity, it expanded congressional authority to all regulation that "affects" such activity. "The power we have accorded Congress has swallowed" the constitutional authority, he observed.[12] Moreover, "[o]ur construction of the scope of congressional authority has the additional problem of coming close to turning the Tenth Amendment on its head," Thomas charged. "Our case law could be read to reserve to the United States all powers not expressly *prohibited* by the Constitution."[13] In that passage, Justice Thomas comes as close as any modern justice to recognizing the presumption of liberty and decentralized authority that animated the Constitution—and clearly he recognizes how far the Court's jurisprudence has removed us from that principle.

Although Justice Thomas recognized that "[c]onsideration of *stare decisis* and reliance interests may convince us that we cannot wipe the slate clean," clearly "we ought to temper our Commerce Clause jurisprudence." The Court's "substantial effects" test—and its efforts to retain rather than to replace it—"is no test at all: It is a blank check."[14]

Five years later in *United States v. Morrison*, when the Court struck down portions of the Violence against Women Act but retained the "substantial effects" test, Justice Thomas warned his colleagues again. "By continuing to apply this rootless and malleable standard, however circumscribed, the Court has encouraged the Federal Government to persist in its view that the Commerce Clause has virtually no limits."[15] His warnings proved prophetic another five years later when the Court retreated from *Lopez* and allowed federal law to trump California's medicinal marijuana statute in *Gonzales v. Raich*. Indeed, a different outcome would have been difficult to square with *Wickard v. Filburn*—which is precisely why Justice Thomas had called upon the Court to reconsider its jurisprudential path rather than to torture it to produce more favorable outcomes. The prosecution at issue in the California case, Justice Thomas noted, involves "marijuana that has never been bought or sold, that has never crossed state lines, and that has had no demonstrable effect on interstate commerce. . . . If Congress can regulate this under the Commerce Clause, then it can regulate virtually anything—and the Federal Government is no longer one of limited and enumerated powers."[16] As Thomas charged: "Federal power expands, and never contracts, with each new locution. The majority is not interpreting the Commerce Clause, but rewriting it."[17]

As if to illustrate in the most glaring way Justice Thomas's point that the Court's commerce clause jurisprudence was sending exactly the wrong signal to the elected branches, Attorney General John Ashcroft, acting on the flimsiest of legal authority, acted unilaterally to overturn by regulatory fiat Oregon's physician-assisted suicide statute. In a 2006 decision, the Court struck down his action, not on any grand Tenth Amendment or commerce clause basis, but on the ground that Ashcroft had exceeded his regulatory authority under relevant federal statutes. In dissent, Justice Scalia (joined by Chief Justice Roberts) abandoned not only his adherence to federalism but also his professed deference to social legislation reflecting the demonstrated will of the people.

Justice Thomas dissented, too, but mainly to make a point. Noting that the Court sweepingly had interpreted the very same federal drug laws while jettisoning federalism principles only a short time earlier in *Raich*, he stated that "[t]oday the majority beats a hasty retreat from these conclusions."[18] Here, Thomas noted, the Court interpreted the statute narrowly to principally encompass concerns about drug abuse, an approach that is "all the more puzzling because it rests on constitutional principles that the majority of the Court rejected in *Raich*," specifically, federalism.[19] "I agree with limiting the applications of the [federal drug laws] in a manner consistent with the principles of federalism," Thomas said, but "that is now water over the dam." He noted that "[s]uch considerations have little, if any, relevance where, as here, we are merely presented with a question of statutory interpretation, and not the extent of constitutionally permissible federal power," and characterized the Court's decision to rehabilitate those principles in the context of interpreting a statute "perplexing to say the least."[20]

The Court's penchant for subjective, results-oriented decisions, which requires an accordion-like expansion and conflation of constitutional principles as circumstances dictate, is not conducive to a consistent rule of law that is the bedrock of a free society. Although there is no sign that the Court's overall proclivities in that regard are coming to an end, at least Justice Thomas is there to make clear what the Court is doing when it strays from a coherent and consistent interpretation of the Constitution and what the natural consequences of its decisions likely will be.

In the more than two decades since I have known Clarence Thomas, one thing that was obvious from the beginning and remains so today is his willingness to stand alone in his beliefs. Fortunately, Justice Thomas often is joined by a majority of his colleagues in protecting individual liberty and enforcing the boundaries of government power, and in examining carefully and applying conscientiously the intent of the Constitution's Framers. But no other justice in recent times goes about the proper enterprise of constitutional interpretation quite so consistently or earnestly as Justice Thomas. Even when he is in the majority, Thomas often is impelled to write separately to criticize the Court for perpetuating doctrines that are incoherent, subjective, and detached from constitutional moorings. Even when he arguably gets it wrong, no one can fault Thomas for not taking seriously his oath to defend and uphold the Constitution and all that oath implies.

Our future as a free society depends in large part on the determination of justices to faithfully apply the rule of law embodied in our Constitution; in that vital role, Clarence Thomas provides a stalwart role model. Let's hope that in future jurisprudence, the word "dissenting" does not follow "Thomas, J." quite so often!

7. Economic Liberty

Leroy Jones perspired under the hot Denver sun, burdened by the heavy tray of Coca-Cola drinks he was attempting to sell to thirsty baseball fans on a summer afternoon. As "The Star-Spangled Banner" sounded over the public address system, Jones paused, removed his cap, and placed a hand over his heart, a tear welling in his eye as he joined the crowd singing our national anthem.

That scene, depicted on CBS's "Eye on America" news report, would seem to portray a man in pursuit of the American Dream. But for Jones, it was a dream denied.

A few years earlier, Jones was earning a living driving a taxi for the ubiquitous Yellow Cabs. But like many people toiling in the employment of others, Jones recognized that the best way to get ahead was to go into business for himself. Jones and three of his fellow drivers, who were African immigrants, discovered a niche in the Five Points section of Denver—a low-income community where taxicab service was in great demand but rarely available. Jones and his colleagues put together a business plan to create a new cooperative company called Quick-Pick Cabs. They had everything they needed: a petition signed by scores of consumers, knowledge of the industry, capital, and insurance. Everything, that is, except a little piece of paper from the Colorado Public Utilities Commission (PUC) called a "certificate of public convenience and necessity."

To obtain the certificate, Jones and his colleagues would have to demonstrate not only that the city's three existing taxicab companies were not serving a particular market—which would present no problem—but also that they *could not* service that market. That requirement was impossible to fulfill. So despite their obvious fitness and the demand for their services, Jones and his colleagues received the same response from the PUC that every other applicant for a taxicab license had received since World War II: application denied. Before long, Jones and his colleagues were fired from Yellow Cabs and forced to pursue other employment to provide for themselves and their families.

Economic liberty—the right to pursue an honest living in a business or profession free from arbitrary government interference—is a right that all Americans possess even though they won't get much help from the courts if the right is violated. As we have seen, if the government denies a person's "right" to a welfare check, that person can tie the government up in legal knots, thanks to inventive Supreme Court decisions. But if government destroys a person's livelihood or business, even for the most nefarious of purposes, courts typically will stand idly by.

That the right to earn an honest living is deemed less fundamental than other rights is bizarre in a nation doctrinally committed to opportunity and freedom of enterprise. After all, freedom of speech and other fundamental liberties matter little if a person cannot earn a living. But ever since that sinister footnote in *Carolene Products* (see chapter 4), economic liberties have been mostly ignored—not just relegated to the status of a poor relative, but thrown out of the family of protected rights altogether.

When my colleagues at the Institute for Justice and I encountered Leroy Jones in the early 1990s, he could not understand how his government could take away with impunity his right to earn a share of the American Dream. Certainly, Jones and his colleagues were no match for Yellow Cabs and its army of lobbyists in the legislative arena. So we took the matter to federal court, which was his only hope.

There, despite the skilled and passionate legal advocacy of my colleague Chip Mellor, we lost. The judge was sympathetic but felt bound by precedent to turn Leroy Jones and his colleagues away empty-handed.

But it was not that court decision that took away Leroy Jones's rights, nor was it the PUC decision denying his permit. Leroy Jones and millions of other American entrepreneurs lost their rights in the century before they were born, in a judicial decision that ranks as one of the most shameful judicial abdications in American history, the *Slaughter-House Cases*.

Most Americans always had enjoyed a great deal of economic liberty. At common law, government-conferred monopolies were unlawful. The one group of Americans who were excluded from such essential liberties were, of course, black slaves. After the Civil War, the victors were determined to invest in the emancipated blacks the most essential civil rights—not just the right to vote, but also economic liberties such as freedom of contract, private property rights, and what they called the right of free labor.

The vanquished were just as determined to negate those rights and thereby to preserve a servile labor supply. Southern states enacted a series of laws called the "Black Codes"—the precursors to the later Jim Crow laws—which restricted or nullified those economic liberties by creating occupational licensing laws, limiting freedom to contract over the terms and conditions of labor, restricting property ownership, and the like.

In response, the Reconstruction Congress, which was imbued with natural-rights principles like no set of legislators since the Founders, enacted the Civil Rights Act of 1866. The law extended to blacks the same rights—freedom of contract and property ownership—as were enjoyed by whites. As Rep. William Lawrence argued, "It is idle to say that a citizen shall have the right to life, yet to deny him the right to labor, whereby alone he can live."[1]

But President Andrew Johnson questioned congressional authority to enact such a law. Wanting to take no such risks, Congress "constitutionalized" the Civil Rights Act of 1866 in the Fourteenth Amendment, which protected the "privileges or immunities" of citizens and due process and equal protection of law.

The Fourteenth Amendment was intended to be a revolutionary enactment, securing to citizens the rights protected by federal law against violations by their own state governments and placing the federal government in a position of primacy in protecting those rights. As a result, the Fourteenth Amendment expanded the privileges and immunities clause from the original Constitution: that clause consistently has been held to protect economic liberty, but only against states that discriminate against citizens of other states (like Juanita Swedenburg in chapter 1). The Fourteenth Amendment, in the words of Sen. Frederick Frelinghuysen, "not merely requires equality of privileges, but it demands that the privileges and immunities of all citizens be absolutely unabridged, unimpaired."[2]

Though the phrase "privileges or immunities" today has an ambiguous meaning, it had a clear and commonly understood meaning to the framers of the Fourteenth Amendment. They frequently cited the broad array of natural rights inherited by American citizens as catalogued by Kent and Blackstone and as sweepingly depicted by

Justice Bushrod Washington in *Corfield v. Coryell*.[3] Sen. John Sherman, one of the amendment's leading architects, defined privileges or immunities to encompass not only the Bill of Rights but also the rights set forth in the Declaration of Independence and protected by common law. Specifically, they encompassed what the principal House author of the Fourteenth Amendment, Rep. John Bingham, described as "the liberty . . . to work in an honest calling and contribute by your toil in some sort to yourself, to the support of your fellowmen, and to be secure in the enjoyment of the fruits of your toil."[4] The framers of the amendment made clear that the rights were not absolute but would be balanced against the state's police power to protect public health, welfare, and morals. But any believer in original intent who devotes even the most cursory attention to the legislative history and to the problem Congress sought to correct will conclude that Congress unambiguously meant to protect economic liberty against excessive state regulation.

But part of the revolution that was won on the battlefield at such human cost and in the halls of Congress was undone by the U.S. Supreme Court. Barely before the ink was dry on the new amendment, a group of Louisiana butchers whose livelihoods were destroyed by a bribery-procured slaughterhouse monopoly went to court to challenge the monopoly charter, which was granted by the legislature, as a violation of the privileges or immunities of citizens.[5] In a 5-4 decision—very unusual during that period—a deeply divided Court in 1873 upheld the monopoly and essentially repealed the privileges or immunities clause by judicial fiat.

Through a remarkable display of semantic ingenuity, Justice Samuel F. Miller concluded for the majority that the privileges or immunities pertained only to those rights derived from national citizenship—such as the right of access to ports and navigable waters, the right to travel from state to state and enjoy the same rights as citizens of those states, and the right of habeas corpus. Although the economic liberty asserted by the butchers did fall within the definition of privileges or immunities, Miller acknowledged, it derived from state citizenship, not federal citizenship, and therefore was subject to protection and regulation by the states.[6] Why the framers of the Fourteenth Amendment would go to such enormous trouble to amend the Constitution to protect that handful of federal citizenship rights, the majority did not venture to speculate.

In dissent, Justice Stephen Field set forth the appropriate role of the courts in challenges to economic regulations: they should defer to proper exercises of the police power, he suggested, but "under the pretense of prescribing a police regulation the State cannot be permitted to encroach upon any of the just rights of citizens, which the Constitution intended to secure against abridgement."[7] The judiciary's task, then, was to look behind the asserted rationale to determine whether the regulation was a proper exercise of police power or a mere pretext. By abdicating that crucial role, Field declared, "the right of free labor, one of the most imprescriptable rights of man, is violated."[8]

Justice Noah H. Swayne, also dissenting, decried the narrow interpretation of the Fourteenth Amendment by the majority. He wrote that the amendment was intended "to rise to the dignity of a new Magna Charta." Proclaiming that "[o]ur duty is to execute the law, not make it," Swayne protested that the majority opinion "defeats, by a limitation not anticipated, the intent of those by whom the amendment was framed." Swayne expressed "hope that the consequences to follow may prove less serious and far-reaching than the minority fear they will be."[9]

But of course those consequences were quite serious and far-reaching. Whenever government is unleashed from its constitutional limits, it is free to indulge the designs of those who exploit its power for their own ends. The most immediate response was the enactment of Jim Crow laws, which relegated blacks to economic servitude and second-class citizenship. When the laws were challenged in *Plessy v. Ferguson*, the challengers were deprived by *Slaughter-House* of their strongest argument, freedom of contract. Instead they were forced to argue on equal protection grounds, which from the standpoint of original intent (given the prevailing practices at the time of the amendment's adoption) was more difficult.[10] The rights intended to be included among the privileges or immunities of citizens— except for those safeguarded by other constitutional provisions— remain unprotected today.[11]

For a period of roughly 50 years between the 1880s and 1930s, a more sympathetic Supreme Court protected economic liberty under the equal protection and due process clauses.[12] In *Yick Wo v. Hopkins*, an 1886 decision that remains good law, the Court struck down on equal protection grounds a San Francisco ordinance that limited laundries to those constructed of brick or stone, a thinly disguised attempt to drive Chinese entrepreneurs out of business. Highlighting the importance of economic liberty, the Court declared that "the very idea that one man may be compelled to hold his life, or the means of living, or any material right essential to the enjoyment of life, at the mere will of another, seems to be intolerable in any country where freedom prevails, as being the essence of slavery itself."[13]

Two decades later, the Court in *Lochner v. New York* invalidated on "substantive" due process grounds a law limiting employment in bakeries to 10 hours per day and 60 hours per week. The majority ruled that the state's police power must be weighed against liberty of contract. "Otherwise the Fourteenth Amendment would have no efficacy and the legislatures of the States would have unbounded power," the Court declared. On the mere assertion that the law was an exercise of police power, "such legislation would be valid, no matter how absolutely without foundation the claim might be."[14] That is, of course, an apt description of the state of the law a century later.

In dissent, the authoritarian Justice Oliver Wendell Holmes proclaimed that "[t]his case is decided upon an economic theory which a large part of the country does not entertain," namely, the "shibboleth" of "[t]he liberty of the citizen to do as he likes so long as he does not interfere with the liberty of others to do the same."[15] In reality, the theory in this case is not an economic one, but a constitutional one. Although the framers of the Fourteenth Amendment may not have intended to protect economic liberty substantively under the due process clause, they did intend to protect it—mainly under the privileges or immunities clause. Hence Holmes was attempting to substitute his own constitutional theory—extreme deference to legislative whims—for the constitutional text and its manifest intent.

The demise of *Lochner* and its progeny came, not surprisingly, in the New Deal era. In *West Coast Hotel Co. v. Parrish*, the Court by a 5-4 vote upheld a minimum wage for women and minors. Declaring that the "Constitution does not speak of freedom of contract" (though actually it does), Chief Justice Charles Evans Hughes revealed the paternalism that underlies many restrictions on economic liberty. The contracting parties were, after all, women, "in whose protection the State has a special interest" owing to their "physical structure and the performance of maternal functions," which renders them "defenseless against the denial of a living wage." (No doubt the decision also left many of them unemployed in the midst of the Great Depression.) Giving voice to his own political philosophy, Chief Justice Hughes ruled that the law was necessary to avoid "a subsidy for unconscionable employers. The community may direct its lawmaking power to correct the abuse which springs from their selfish disregard for the public interest."[16]

In dissent, Justice George Sutherland argued in vain that the economic crisis did not justify abrogating the Constitution. Far from creating an absolute rule, the Court's precedents merely established that "freedom of contract was the general rule and restraint the exception; and that the power to abridge that freedom could only be justified by the existence of exceptional circumstances"[17]—in other words, the constitutional presumption of liberty that the Framers intended.

Regardless of whether the outcome in *West Coast Hotel* was correct, its doctrine of nearly complete deference to legislative power spelled the death knell for judicial protection of economic liberty. *Lochner* became a universal pejorative, among both liberals and conservatives.

Because of the Court's wrong-headed jurisprudence, the real-world consequences have been severe. In 1976, the Court in *City of New Orleans v. Dukes* unanimously upheld a New Orleans ordinance limiting the number of vendor pushcarts in the French Quarter to two, wiping out a competitor's business. In the sphere of economic regulation, the Court held, "it is only the invidious discrimination, the wholly arbitrary act, which cannot stand consistently with the Fourteenth Amendment."[18]

The Court's abdication of its duty to protect economic liberty reached its peak in 1993 in a decision written by, distressingly, Justice Clarence Thomas. In *FCC v. Beach Communications*, the Court considered a federal statute that subjected satellite master-antenna systems to local franchising laws while exempting small cable television providers. No justification was given for the differential treatment, yet the Court unanimously upheld the rule. Under the rational basis standard, Justice Thomas wrote, a statute "comes before us bearing a strong presumption of validity," and "those attacking the rationality of the legislative classification have the burden 'to negative every conceivable basis which might support it.'"[19] Moreover, "because we never require a legislature to articulate its reasons

for enacting a statute, it is entirely irrelevant for constitutional purposes whether the conceived reason for the challenged distinction
actually motivated the legislature." As a result, "a legislative choice
is not subject to courtroom factfinding and may be based on rational
speculation unsupported by evidence or empirical data." All of that
renders the "legislative judgment virtually unreviewable, since the
legislature must be allowed leeway to approach a perceived problem
incrementally."[20] Clearly that was not what the framers of the Fourteenth Amendment had in mind.

But that was the daunting jurisprudential backdrop I faced in the
mid-1980s when I hung up a public interest law shingle in a town-
house basement across from the U.S. Supreme Court with goals
only an inexperienced and precocious young lawyer could have: to
overturn the *Slaughter-House Cases* and restore economic liberty as
a fundamental civil right. I had a strategy: to stitch together the few
strands of favorable remaining economic liberty jurisprudence—
Yick Wo and a handful of other somewhat analogous cases—and
find a compelling case in which to apply them, with the goal of
building some positive case law until such time as the Supreme
Court would reconsider *Slaughter-House*.

Around that time, I wrote my first two books, *Changing Course*
(1988) and *Unfinished Business* (1990), which sketched an outline for
such a legal strategy. Fortunately, I was not alone in my views on
the privileges or immunities clause: scholars such as Bernard Siegan,
Charles Lofgren, and Michael Kent Curtis were questioning the
underpinnings of *Slaughter-House*. And the Bradley Foundation saw
fit to provide seed funding to give my humble public interest law
endeavor a try. All that remained was to find the perfect case.

I found it, of all places, in the pages of the *Washington Post Magazine*. A feature story described the plight of Ego Brown, whose
outdoor shoeshine stand at the corner of 19th and M Streets had
been shut down by the District police. The article recounted that
Brown, an aspiring entrepreneur whose flamboyant shoeshine style
had attracted not only a stream of customers but also franchisees
from the ranks of the District's enterprising homeless population,
had run into an old Jim Crow–era law that forbade "bootblacks"
from plying their craft on the public streets. One could sell almost
anything on the streets of our nation's capital, from hot dogs to
photo opportunities with cardboard Al Gores, but not shoeshines.

When I met Ego Brown, he was toiling indoors, shining shoes at a hotel. I told him that I thought his constitutional rights had been violated and that I was willing to file a lawsuit on his behalf, though the odds of success admittedly were against us. He readily agreed, and we went on to make sweet litigation together.

Soon Ego Brown was facing dire economic circumstances. The hotel in which he was shining shoes closed for renovations. In the midst of winter, the utility company was threatening to turn off his heat. I sought a preliminary injunction from the court, but it was denied. My friend Bob Woodson, president of the National Center for Neighborhood Enterprise, knew exactly what to do: he threw a rent party that helped Ego make it through the winter.

Fortunately, we were up against the District of Columbia, whose lawyers refused to provide any justification for the law because, in their view, doing so was unnecessary. And on the first day of spring in 1989, the federal district court struck down the law as a violation of the due process clause of the Fifth Amendment.[21] The court declared that "the rational basis test requires that the justification posited by the legislature be *both* conceivable and rational."[22] Specifically, "[t]here must be at least some plausible connection between the 'uniqueness' of a bootblack and the purpose of the law." In this case, the "inability of the District to articulate any rational basis for distinguishing bootblacks from other types of vendors combined with the regulation's elusive purpose compel us to declare this regulation unconstitutional."[23]

The Ego Brown case became the first building block in the campaign to restore economic liberty as a fundamental civil right. Five years later, a second was added. A Houston entrepreneur, Alfredo Santos, wanted to use his off-duty taxicab to operate a "jitney" service on a main thoroughfare. The jitney would charge a flat fee for pickup and discharge anywhere along the route. Jitneys are a mainstay of public transportation in many Latin American countries (where they are called *peseros*). Like buses, they operate along a fixed route for a flat fee but are more flexible in terms of pickup and drop-off; unlike public buses, they are unsubsidized, but they are cheaper than taxicabs.

In America in the early part of the 20th century, jitneys flourished in many major cities. Their main competitors were streetcars, whose owners succeeded in having the jitneys outlawed nearly everywhere, including Houston. Seventy years later, the streetcars had disappeared from most cities, but the protectionist laws remained, kept in place for the benefit of unionized and often highly inefficient public transit systems.

The federal district court struck down Houston's Anti-Jitney Law of 1924 under the rational basis standard. "The purpose of the statute was economic protectionism in its most glaring form," Judge John D. Rainey found, "and this goal was not legitimate."[24] Moreover, even if the goal was legitimate, "the ordinance has outlived its ill-begotten existence."[25] As a result, the law flunked both parts of the ends/means test and therefore violated the Fourteenth Amendment.

Around the same time I was litigating the *Santos* case, I met a man with another compelling economic liberty story. Taalib-din Uqdah and his wife Pamela Ferrell were operating a salon in the District of Columbia called Cornrows & Co. The salon engaged exclusively in the centuries-old craft of African hairstyling, using highly specialized skills, such as braiding, cornrowing, and weaving. The salon served an upscale clientele, hiring and training stylists from the ranks of the unemployed.

But in our nation's capital, no good deed goes unpunished, and District police officers closed the salon. The heinous crime? Braiding hair without a cosmetology license. In Washington, D.C., and most states at that time, anyone engaged in any business involving hairstyling had to pass a barbering or cosmetology examination. The rules were set by the Board of Cosmetology, most of whose members were licensed in the profession and possessed of an interest in limiting the number of competitors. To sit for the test, applicants had to take 1,600 hours of training—more than a police officer or emergency medical technician—in a licensed cosmetology school. The instruction and testing required extensive proficiency in the use of chemicals in the hair, eyebrow arching, cosmetics, manicuring, and obsolete white hair styles—none of which African hairstylists used or performed. The only skill the applicants did not need to exhibit any proficiency in whatsoever was braiding hair.

As a result of such ridiculous laws, most African hairstylists operated unlawfully—thereby defeating any professed governmental concern for public health and safety. When a salon such as Cornrows & Co. dared to operate in the light of day, it risked being shut down.

We challenged the District's cosmetology licensing laws in federal court—and lost. Though the judge was sympathetic—he compared the licensing regime to Soviet Russia, to which I responded that I might seek economic asylum for my clients in Russia because their markets were more free than America's—he concluded that the law required him to turn Uqdah and Ferrell away with no relief.

Fortunately we litigated the case not only in the court of law but also in the court of public opinion, where the verdict was far more favorable. In particular, a brilliant exposeé on the District's cosmetology cartel by John Stossel on ABC's *20/20* titled "Rules, Rules, Stupid Rules" managed to shame the city's officials, who deregulated African hairstyling. Whereas only one salon existed before the law was changed, I am told that more than 75 African hairstyling salons exist in the capital city today.

But Uqdah wasn't done. He created a trade association and launched a crusade to deregulate African hairstyling across the nation. Several legislatures did so voluntarily, but others did not. So we filed a second lawsuit, this time in California—and won.

The plaintiff was Dr. Joanne Cornwell, chair of the African Studies Department at San Diego State University and creator of a hairstyling technique called Sisterlocks. Under California's oppressive licensing regime, she was considered an outlaw.

In California, the cartel decided to make its stand, and it brought out the industry's big guns to justify the regulatory regime. Federal district court judge Rudi M. Brewster didn't buy the rationale. His 1999 ruling declared that under the rational basis test, "[t]here must be some congruity between the means employed and the stated end or the test would be a nullity."[26] Sifting meticulously through the regulations, curriculum, and examination, the court could not find the required nexus. Only a tiny fraction of the required instruction related to services provided or skills needed by African hairstylists. Indeed, "forcing African hair braiders to attend cosmetology school logically impedes their ability to offer competent hair-braiding services to their customers, i.e., it leaves them untrained to perform their own craft."[27] The powerful *Cornwell* precedent has induced other states to reduce barriers to entry into the African hairstyling profession.

Another cartel that uses the force of law to protect its sheltered status is the funeral industry. In Tennessee, the Rev. Nathaniel Craigmiles was incensed over the exorbitant prices his congregants were forced to pay by funeral homes for caskets. So he started a store to sell caskets and urns at prices far below the markups charged by the funeral homes.

The business quickly was shut down by the Board of Funeral Directors and Embalmers under a state law that gave licensed funeral directors a monopoly over the sale of caskets and urns. To secure a funeral director's license, one must undergo extensive training and apprenticeship, including the embalming of corpses. Little of the prescribed training related to the sale of caskets and urns. When the Institute for Justice challenged the law, the state asserted health and safety justifications, such as postburial seepage of fluids from caskets. But Tennessee law did not require burial in a casket at all, so the justification appeared obviously pretextual. Indeed, Reverend Craigmiles sold the exact same caskets as the funeral homes, except at a much lower price. That, of course, was exactly the point: his business interfered with the artificial monopoly profits extracted by funeral homes during times of enormous grief and stress.

The law was struck down as a violation of the Fourteenth Amendment by the U.S. Court of Appeals for the Sixth Circuit in 2002. "Finding no rational relationship to any of the articulated purposes of the state," wrote Judge Danny J. Boggs, "we are left to the more obvious illegitimate purpose to which licensure provision is very well tailored." Specifically, the law "imposes a significant barrier to competition in the casket market," which in turn "harms consumers in their pocketbooks."[28]

The Court was "not imposing our view of a well-functioning market on the people of Tennessee," but merely was invalidating the "naked attempt to raise a fortress protecting the monopoly rents that funeral directors extract from consumers." A law "to privilege certain businessmen over others at the expense of consumers is not animated by a legitimate governmental purpose and cannot survive even rational basis review."[29]

The Institute for Justice filed a similar claim against an Oklahoma casket monopoly scheme, but the 10th Circuit's decision upholding the law two years later could not have reached a more starkly opposite conclusion. The court was nearly as dubious as the Sixth Circuit about the alleged connection between the state's asserted objectives and the law's sweep. But it considered legally irrelevant the possibility that the law was adopted for protectionist purposes, because "protecting or favoring one intrastate industry, absent a specific federal constitutional or statutory violation, is a legitimate state interest."[30]

That assertion is truly extraordinary. Notice the tacit acknowledgment that if the state had erected a similar barrier against *interstate* trade (as in the case of Juanita Swedenburg), it would be unconstitutional. But states are free to impose such barriers to economic liberty upon their own citizens. Given that the purpose of the Fourteenth Amendment was to extend federal constitutional rights to citizens against their own state governments, the 10th Circuit ruling illustrates how empty that constitutional vessel has become. Moreover, what is the specific constitutional provision that would protect citizens against interstate trade barriers? The commerce clause and the privileges or immunities clause do. But, thanks to the *Slaughter-House Cases*, the Fourteenth Amendment's privileges or immunities clause somehow is not sufficiently specific to curtail overtly protectionist trade barriers within a state.

The 10th Circuit noted that "while baseball may be the national pastime, dishing out special economic benefits to certain in-state industries remains the favorite pastime of state and local governments." But "adopting a rule against the legitimacy of intrastate economic protectionism and applying it in a principled manner would have wide-ranging economic consequences." Indeed, "besides the threat to all licensed professions such as doctors, teachers, accountants, plumbers, and lawyers," (oh no, not *lawyers!*), "every piece of legislation . . . aiming to protect or favor one industry or another in the hopes of luring jobs to that state would be in danger." The court concluded, "While the creation of such a libertarian paradise may be a worthy goal, Plaintiffs must turn to the Oklahoma electorate for its institution, not us."[31]

Wish it or not, the proper application of rational basis scrutiny to economic regulations would not create a libertarian paradise. If a state could articulate a legitimate police-power justification, such as public health or safety, and demonstrate that the law actually is related in a rational way to that objective, the law would be sustained. That such a standard would imperil many regulations of entry into businesses and professions is not a caution against aggressive judicial action but instead is powerful evidence of how far governments have overstepped their constitutional bounds. Moreover, the rule of law derided by the 10th Circuit was precisely what the Framers of the original Constitution sought when they attempted to curb the evil of protectionist legislation procured by factions and what the framers of the Fourteenth Amendment sought to create through the protection of the privileges or immunities of citizens. As Justice Stephen Field declared in his *Slaughter-House* dissent, "That only is a free government, in the American sense of the term, under which the inalienable right of every citizen to pursue his happiness is unrestrained, except by just, equal, and impartial laws."[32] How far we have strayed from that understanding.

Ordinarily, a clear and complete conflict of authority such as presented by the opinions of the Sixth and 10th Circuits would trigger review by the U.S. Supreme Court. But the Court declined to review the Oklahoma decision, leaving would-be entrepreneurs to the mercy of subjective judicial proclivities. Perhaps the Court is not yet ready to reconsider the damage done by the *Slaughter-House Cases* over a quarter and a century ago. As Antonin Scalia remarked about such an enterprise some time ago: "The task of creating what I might call a constitutional ethos of economic liberty is no easy one. But it is the first task."[33]

That task falls to courageous entrepreneurs such as Ego Brown, Taalib-din Uqdah and Pamela Ferrell, Alfredo Santos, Leroy Jones, and Nathaniel Craigmiles. I did not finish the story of Leroy Jones earlier. Thanks to national publicity, while the adverse district court ruling was pending on appeal, the state capitulated and deregulated entry into the taxicab industry.[34] But along the way, in the darkest days when his dream of owning his own business seemed hopelessly remote, Leroy Jones had an epiphany. His struggle was not just about Quick-Pick Cabs and the Denver taxicab market. It was much bigger than that: it symbolized the broader struggle to earn a share of the American Dream.

So Jones and his partners renamed their enterprise Freedom Cabs. And today, thanks to the courage and perspicacity of Jones and his partners (but no thanks to the courts), a fleet of 75 cabs proudly bearing the insignia of Freedom Cabs operates on the streets of Denver.

Sadly, few struggles against economic protectionism end up that way. Indeed, few in Jones's situation can avail themselves of the limited legal resources arrayed against the leviathan of government oppression, much less the public relations campaign that ultimately brought down the Colorado law.[35] Americans should not have to go to such lengths to secure the essential liberties that are their birthright. If more courts start fulfilling their constitutional duty in the realm of economic liberty, maybe we won't have to.

8. Private Property Rights

The *New York Times* recently reported on the sad plight of a community of farmers whose land was being seized by the local government. The powers that be, it seemed, had decided that the land would be better put to use as factories. The farmers' leases were essentially torn up, notwithstanding the constitutional guarantee of sanctity of contract. But as one local leader assured everyone, "All the proper procedures were carried out." As a result, the fields were bulldozed and people who had farmed land in the countryside their entire lives were compelled to move to the city in an attempt to find work. Some were reduced to collecting and selling garbage.[1]

Not surprisingly, the events I've just described took place in Communist China. One would expect that in a totalitarian country with little respect for property rights or the rule of law, bureaucrats could seize land from one person and give it to another with impunity.

But certainly not in the United States, right? Not only do we have a rich tradition of private property rights, but those rights are expressly protected in the U.S. Constitution.[2] Both the Fifth and Fourteenth Amendments clothe property rights with the guarantee of due process. Even more to the point, the Fifth Amendment states, "nor shall private property be taken for public use, without just compensation."

At least that is what Susette Kelo and her neighbors in the Fort Trumbull area of New London, Connecticut, thought until they received a rude awakening. Kelo had lived in her home with its view of the water since 1997 and had made extensive improvements to it. Her neighbor Wilhelmina Dery had lived in her home since she was born in 1918, and her husband took up residence there when they were married more than 60 years ago. Their son lived in the next-door house, which he and his wife received as a wedding gift. The neighborhood was a tidy and close-knit one, comprising residences and small businesses—a true slice of America.

But in the late 1990s, as part of a broader plan to redevelop New London and increase its tax base, the New London Development

Corporation, a private nonprofit organization invested with the power of eminent domain, decided to initiate proceedings to raze most of the Fort Trumbull neighborhood. The purposes were nebulous. Pfizer Corporation had announced plans to locate a research facility adjacent to Fort Trumbull. The planners wanted the Fort Trumbull property to support a new nearby marina and complement the Pfizer effort by providing research and development office space, retail, and parking lots.

Kelo and the Derys did not want to move. Nor should they have been forced to. Traditionally, the awesome power of eminent domain has been limited to the construction of public facilities, such as roads, schools, hospitals, and the like—hence the explicit limitation of the power in the Fifth Amendment to public use. This condemnation, by contrast, involved the taking of land to transfer from one private owner to another. When Kelo and her neighbors went to court to try to stop the condemnation, however, they were turned away without relief. Economic development, the state courts reasoned, conferred a public *benefit*, and therefore was constitutionally permissible.

Such instances of naked corporate welfare—of Robin Hood in reverse, taking from the poor to give to the wealthy and politically powerful—have become increasingly commonplace across the American landscape. My Institute for Justice colleague Dana Berliner was able to document more than 10,000 cases over a five-year period in which the eminent domain power was threatened or used to take property from one private owner to give to another.[3] Many of the entities exercising the power are not democratically accountable to anyone. As if the expropriation of property for the benefit of private interests were not enough, such abuses of eminent domain often are accompanied by lavish subsidies to the new owners. Moreover, the legal rules are rigged against the current property owners: because most legal fees in eminent domain cases are paid out of compensation awards, few homeowners or small-business owners have the means to fight over whether government has the power to take the property in the first place.

As with many other contemporary instances of government tyranny, the path was cleared of constitutional obstacles many years earlier. In 1954—ironically, the same year that the U.S. Supreme Court launched a crusade for educational freedom—the Court eviscerated an essential constitutional protection of private property rights. In *Berman v. Parker*, the owners of a department store objected to the taking of their property as part of a slum clearance project in the District of Columbia. Their property was not blighted, its taking was unnecessary for slum clearance, and the property would be given to a different business owner. For all those reasons, they argued, the taking was not for a public use.

The Court, in a unanimous opinion written by Justice William O. Douglas, declared that the eminent domain power was not limited strictly to public use but could be used to advance the "public welfare," a concept that "is broad and inclusive." Douglas waxed positively lyrical about the power to advance public welfare. "The values it represents are spiritual as well as physical, aesthetic as well as monetary. It is within the power of the legislature to determine that the community should be beautiful as well as healthy, spacious as well as clean, well-balanced as well as carefully patrolled."[4]

Even if one were to buy Justice Douglas's romanticizing, using the government's regulatory power to advance public welfare is one thing; doing so by means of eminent domain, whose deployment is constitutionally circumscribed, is quite another. But the Court saw it differently. "Once the object is within the power of Congress, the right to realize it through the exercise of eminent domain is clear." Douglas noted that the project involves "a taking from one businessman for the benefit of another businessman. But the means of executing the project are for Congress and Congress alone to determine, once the public purpose has been established."[5]

Note the truly grandiose sweep of the *Berman* decision. It transforms a Constitution of limited and defined powers into one of unlimited power. It gives effect to the clear manipulation of government power in order to benefit some to the detriment of others. It literally repeals an express guarantee of the Constitution, substituting the word "use" with "purpose" or "welfare." And it does so *without a single dissent*. If ever a precedent were undeserving of the protection of *stare decisis*, this surely is it.

Yet even in the waning days of the Rehnquist Court, making a serious dent in the Court's eminent domain jurisprudence proved impossible. The road to *Kelo* was paved through Hawaii, which in the 1980s decided to effectuate a mass redistribution of land ownership. Tracing back to the days of native hegemony, land in

Hawaii was concentrated in the hands of a relatively few owners. So the state decided to condemn parcels of property in order to transfer title from the owners to the tenants. The scheme was breathtaking in scope, yet upheld once again by a unanimous decision of the U.S. Supreme Court, *Hawaii Housing Authority v. Midkiff*—in 1984, appropriately enough, given its Orwellian overtones.

The decision by Justice Sandra Day O'Connor declared, "In short, the Court has made it clear that it will not substitute its judgment for a legislature's judgment as to what constitutes a public use 'unless the use be palpably without reasonable foundation.'"[6] And what could be more palpably reasonable than reducing "the perceived social and economic evils of a land oligopoly traceable to . . . monarchs"?[7] The Court noted reassuringly that a "purely private taking could not withstand the scrutiny of the public use requirement." But the legislature here used eminent domain "not to benefit a particular class of identifiable individuals but to attack certain perceived evils of concentrated property ownership in Hawaii—a legitimate public purpose."[8] But of course that simply isn't so: the property was taken from one distinct class, large landowners, and transferred to another distinct class with identifiable members, their tenants. Once again, the Constitution was rewritten, to replace "public use" with "public purpose"—the ultimate catch-all given that even when government acts tyrannically, it always has a purpose.

So it is perhaps little wonder that when Susette Kelo and her neighbors took their case to the U.S. Supreme Court in 2005, they came away empty-handed. To be sure, the equities were quite different than in *Midkiff*, for the property was taken not from the rich to be redistributed to the poor, but from working-class people to give to wealthy developers. Still, as if to illustrate the consequences of abandoning the rule of law, *Midkiff* proved to be an unworkable precedent even to its author, Justice O'Connor. In *Kelo*, she wrote a passionate dissent in a 5-4 decision.

The majority decision in *Kelo* was written by Justice John Paul Stevens, joined by Justices Anthony Kennedy, David Souter, Ruth Bader Ginsburg, and Stephen Breyer. The swing vote by Justice Kennedy was especially disappointing, for previously he had exhibited a keen understanding of the centrality of private property rights in the American constitutional system, proclaiming in one case the "essential principle" that "[i]ndividual freedom finds tangible expression in property rights."[9]

If the majority did not have the Constitution on its side, it certainly had abundant contemporary precedent. Giving lip service to the notion that the city could not "take property under the mere pretext of a public purpose, when its actual purpose was to bestow a private benefit," the Court found that the takings in this case were "executed pursuant to a 'carefully considered' development plan."[10] Or, to paraphrase the Chinese official, all of the proper paperwork was completed. The Court acknowledged that early American jurisprudence recognized that public use meant public use, but "that narrow view steadily eroded over time," because "it proved to be impractical given the diverse and always evolving needs of society."[11] Of course, the proper way to change the meaning of the Constitution when its rules become impractical is spelled out by the Constitution itself, but amendment by judicial fiat is so much simpler and more efficient. The case, the majority ruled, turned on whether the taking was for a "public purpose," and "our cases have defined that concept broadly, reflecting our longstanding policy of deference to legislative judgments in this field."[12]

Saving one of her best for one of her final opinions, Justice O'Connor dissented, joined by Rehnquist, Scalia, and Thomas. "When interpreting the Constitution," she declared, "we begin with the unremarkable presumption that every word has independent meaning."[13] That includes both "public use" and "just compensation." Together, those two provisions "ensure stable property ownership by providing safeguards against excessive, unpredictable, or unfair use of the government's eminent domain power—particularly against owners who, for whatever reasons, may be unable to protect themselves in the political process against the majority's will."[14] O'Connor went on to distinguish previous cases by finding that "New London does not claim that Susette Kelo's and Wilhelmina Dery's well-maintained homes are the source of any social harm."[15] Moreover, economic development alone cannot stand as a justification for eminent domain, because "if predicted (or even guaranteed) positive side-effects"—such as "increased tax revenue, more jobs, maybe even aesthetic pleasure"—"are enough to render transfer from one private party to another constitutional, then the words 'for public use' do not realistically exclude *any* takings, and thus do not exert any constraint on the eminent domain power."[16]

O'Connor was impelled to acknowledge, with understatement, that "[t]here is a sense in which this troubling result follows from the errant language in *Berman* and *Midkiff*."[17] But she drew the line in *Kelo* and finished her dissent with considerable rhetorical flourish. "Any property may now be taken for the benefit of another private party, but the fallout from this decision will not be random," she observed, for "the government now has license to transfer property from those with fewer resources to those with more. The Founders cannot have intended this perverse result."[18]

For Justice Thomas, the decision was an abomination of original constitutional intent—but also, once again, the logical extension of decades of judicial abdication. The plain meaning and history of the takings clause—dating back to William Blackstone, whose views the Framers sought to incorporate in the Constitution—clearly proscribed takings for private use. "I do not believe that this Court can eliminate liberties expressly enumerated in the Constitution," he declared. The ruling "is simply the latest in a string of our cases construing the Public Use Clause to be a virtual nullity, without the slightest nod to its original meaning."[19]

Thomas found that the term "public use" had a clear meaning at the time of the founding and in common law, encompassing property owned by the government or where the public had a legal right to use it. By contrast, mere "public purpose" is a nebulous standard with no constitutional basis.

Thomas attacked the topsy-turvy world of property rights jurisprudence. "[I]t is backward to adopt a searching standard of constitutional review for nontraditional property interests, such as welfare benefits," he charged, "while deferring to the legislature's determination as to what constitutes a public use when it exercises the power of eminent domain, and thereby invades individuals' traditional rights in real property."[20] Moreover, the burden of eminent domain for economic redevelopment "will fall disproportionately on poor communities," which are "not only systematically less likely to put their lands to the highest and best social use, but are also the least politically powerful," he observed. "If ever there were justification for intrusive judicial review of constitutional provisions that protect 'discrete and insular minorities,'" Thomas argued, "surely that principle would apply with great force to the powerless groups and individuals the Public Use Clause protects. The deferential standard this Court has adopted for the Public Use Clause is therefore deeply perverse."[21]

Thomas's point is telling: ironically, the liberal justices who voted in the *Kelo* majority would protect discrete and insular minorities only in the exercise of rights the justices find worthwhile—which apparently does not include property ownership. Surely, most people of modest means aspiring to a share of the American Dream would beg to differ with the values of the majority justices and embrace the greater value assigned to property ownership by the Constitution's Framers.

Though most conservatives appear to agree with Justice Thomas that *Kelo*, and the jurisprudence that preceded it, is an abomination in terms of original intent, the case offers a cautionary tale of how conservative prescriptions for judicial inaction would eviscerate precious liberties. Case Western University law professor Jonathan Adler, for instance, defended *Kelo* in terms reminiscent of Robert Bork. Despite "accepting that the phrase 'public use' places some limitation on the use of eminent domain," Adler argues, "it is not clear what that limit is."[22] Does it mean property that the public can use? Or property placed under government ownership? Because the meaning is "imprecise," Adler asserts, it is improper for the courts to give it any meaning at all. So that even though the use to which New London sought to put the property clearly was not public by any conceivable sense of the term, but instead was justified only as serving a public purpose, the clause places no constraint whatsoever on government power. That is the illogical but necessary consequence of following the most extreme conservatives down the path of judicial abdication.

The real-world backlash from the *Kelo* decision has had a vehemence rarely seen outside of issues like abortion or desegregation—except that in this instance, the intense and widespread antipathy toward the decision is shared on both sides of the ideological divide. Conservatives view eminent domain abuse as a profound violation of private property rights; liberals view it as a particularly pernicious form of corporate welfare; and libertarians realize that they're both right. As an ironic result, the practical effect of a bad decision may turn out to be better than a narrow favorable decision would have been, for popular outrage has translated into a wave of state legislation designed to put clamps on eminent domain abuse.[23] Of course, people should not have to take democratic action to protect rights that already exist—but the spectacle of such action to push back a pendulum that has swung too far in the direction of government power is a reaffirmation of the enduring spirit of American liberty.

One manifestation of popular outrage against the *Kelo* decision was a widely publicized attempt by citizens in Justice Souter's hometown in New Hampshire to take his home and turn it into a higher, revenue-generating use, namely the Lost Liberty Hotel.[24] Even Supreme Court justices who do not protect other people's rights are entitled to their own rights, and ultimately his fellow townspeople decided not to use the eminent domain power that Justice Souter and four of his colleagues had entrusted to them. If only other local government officials exercised such noble self-restraint! In any case, special-interest groups—especially local governments with their taxpayer-funded armies of lobbyists—are sure to squelch most of the efforts to curb eminent domain abuse, meaning that state and federal constitutional action remains essential.

The justices may be getting the message, however. In one of the first decisions in the term following *Kelo*, the Court by a 5-3 vote struck down the warrantless search of a home where permission for the police to enter was denied by the occupant but granted by his estranged wife. The same five justices who voted to uphold the nullification of property rights in *Kelo* decided in this instance that the police had gone too far in invading the sanctity of the man's home. What was much more surprising was their rhetoric, which would have come in handy in *Kelo*. "We have, after all," observed the justices in an opinion by Justice Stevens, "lived our whole national history with an understanding of 'the ancient adage that a man's home is his castle.'"[25] If only the justices grasped that understanding a bit more consistently—and recognized that it is rooted not only in the Fourth Amendment's protection against warrantless searches, but also in the Fifth Amendment's takings clause.

Although the Court continues to view the public use limitation as having been written in disappearing ink, it still can vaguely perceive the second half of the takings clause: the "just compensation" requirement. Generally (though not always) the Court has stood firm that when the government actually takes property—even a little bit of it, and even for a temporary period—it must compensate the owner. Of course, the local government can determine the rules of property use at the outset—such as through zoning—and combat harm to others without paying compensation.

But what if government regulates property, for some broad public purpose, so severely as to divest the property owner of one of the attributes of property ownership (such as the right to convey or use the property, or to exclude others from using it)? What if the regulation significantly reduces the economic value of the property? And what if the rules of the game are changed after the property owner has acquired reasonable expectations about the permissible uses or value of the property? The government does that all the time, trying to accomplish perceived social ends without footing the bill. In such circumstances, is imposing the entire burden upon the individual property owner fair, or should the broader society that presumably reaps the benefits carry the primary burden? To ask the question is to answer it, and both the due process and the takings clauses compel just compensation.

For a long time the Court acknowledged that a regulation could constitute a taking if it "goes too far."[26] But it took the Rehnquist Court to identify instances in which government regulations were so burdensome that compensation to the property owners was constitutionally compelled.

In *Nollan v. California Coastal Commission* in 1987, the Court reviewed a commission order that decreed that the owners of a beachfront lot could replace a small bungalow with a larger house only if they agreed to grant a public easement across their beach, which was located between two public beaches. The Court ruled that the commission's justifications—protecting the public's ability to see the beach, overcoming a "psychological barrier" to using the public beaches, and preventing beach congestion—were pretextual. Accordingly, if the government wanted an easement, the government would have to pay for it.

The government may impose reasonable conditions upon development, Justice Scalia wrote for a 5-4 majority, but the "evident constitutional propriety disappears . . . if the condition . . . utterly fails to further the end advanced as the justification."[27] That "essential nexus" must be established by the government by showing that the condition substantially advances a legitimate public interest—a much weightier burden than the "rational basis" standard. "The Commission may well be right that [public access] is a good idea," Scalia observed, "but that does not establish that the Nollans . . . alone can be compelled to contribute to its realization."[28]

Five years later, a case from the opposite coast but with a similar story of government abuse came before the Court. David Lucas bought two beachfront lots, intending to build homes in accord with the applicable zoning. But the South Carolina Coastal Council, ostensibly in an effort to prevent beach erosion, decided to prohibit further development, thereby reducing the value of the property from over a million dollars to less than zero. (Poor David Lucas still had to pay property taxes even though he could do nothing with the property.) The government had not formally exercised its eminent domain power, but for all intents and purposes, it had taken the property: the Coastal Council wanted open, undeveloped land, and it accomplished that goal not by seizing ownership and compensating the owner but by forbidding David Lucas from developing his property. The constitutional question presented was whether that amounted to a de facto taking. In more practical terms, the question before the Court was whether David Lucas alone could be forced to bear the costs of the Coastal Council's desires, or whether they should be shared more broadly.

In *Lucas*, the Court by a 5-4 vote, with Justice Scalia writing for the majority, decided that finally it had seen a regulation that went too far, denying the property owner all economically viable use of his property. Had the council regulated a use that the owner did not have a right to in the first place—like committing a nuisance—that would not constitute a taking. But where the regulation amounted to a confiscatory land use measure, the government would have to pay.[29]

Ironically, when South Carolina was forced to pay Lucas for the value of his property, the state decided that its professed environmental concerns weren't so important after all, and it turned around and sold the property—to a developer. It is enlightening to see how rationally government can act when it has to bear the costs of its own regulations.

The renaissance for private property rights hit its zenith—at least during the Rehnquist era—in a case two years following *Lucas* involving an elderly widow named Florence Dolan who wanted to expand her hardware store in Tigard, Oregon. That's fine, said the city, but first you'll have to construct a bicycle path and cede to the city a public greenway along the riverbank. Mrs. Dolan considered the city's demand extortionist. Fortunately, a 5-4 majority of the U.S. Supreme Court agreed.

Imposing upon a property owner as a condition of a development permit the costs of the proposed development upon a community is quite permissible. A new housing development, for instance, might be called upon to contribute to building roads or a school to serve the development. But a bicycle path and a greenway as a condition of expanding a hardware store? Not too many people make their hardware purchases aboard an unmotorized two-wheeler. Writing for the majority, Chief Justice Rehnquist demanded that the city show a "rough proportionality" between the exaction demanded in exchange for the permit and the "nature and extent [of] the impact of the proposed development."[30] In Mrs. Dolan's case, the city's desire was clearly to have the property owner subsidize some desired goodies, which had little if any connection to the impact of the proposed expansion.

As a result of such decisions, property owners now have some recourse against excessive government regulations of their property. But government still holds far too many of the cards. Governments have especially exploited two loopholes in the Court's decisions. First, in *Lucas*, the Court found that a regulation depriving a property owner of *all* economically viable use of the property constitutes a compensable taking. So governments now are sure to leave a negligible amount of value—say 5 or 10 percent. The Court still has not resolved the question of whether such regulations can amount to takings. The one case in which it addressed the question left the issue murky. In *Palazzolo v. Rhode Island*, the Court in 2001 ruled that where regulators refused to allow a property owner to fill in wetlands in order to build a beach club, the prohibition did not amount to complete diminution in the value of the property because they left him the right to construct a residence on the 18-acre parcel. The Court ruled that to avoid a taking the government must leave more than a token amount of value—but whether the remaining value need be truly substantial or only a smidgen was left unresolved.[31] In the meantime, property owners are suffering grievous losses. Many confiscatory development exactions are unchallenged, especially because developers know their livelihoods depend upon the good graces of governmental officials, so the cost/benefit analysis rarely tips in favor of legal challenges. The resulting added costs, of course, are passed along to homebuyers, and the stock of affordable housing is diminished.

A second loophole is the doctrine of "ripeness." A property owner cannot challenge a regulation until the government decision is "final." No matter how many layers of bureaucracy a property owner must endure, until all of them have had their say there can be no lawsuit for a taking. So if government wants to limit development, it need not deny a permit and thereby possibly trigger compensation. Instead, it simply defers a decision—if necessary, forever.

I believe such conduct violates due process—not because the government is providing too little of it, but too much. In essence, the process itself is the violation, for by subjecting property owners to endless process, they are denied constitutional rights without judicial recourse. To date, the Court has not considered such a claim.

But the Court did make short work of a related claim—and put an end to the Rehnquist-era property rights revolution—in its 2002 decision in the Lake Tahoe case. Property owners challenged two moratoria, totaling 32 months (and counting), imposed by the Tahoe Regional Planning Agency, that stifled all development while the agency supposedly was formulating a comprehensive land-use plan. By a 6-3 vote, the Court ruled that the moratoria on their face did not constitute a per se taking requiring compensation.

The majority opinion by Justice Stevens held that a "rule that required compensation for every delay in the use of property would render routine government processes prohibitively expensive or encourage hasty decisionmaking."[32] The Court's concerns are with the wrong party. The property owner has a right under existing zoning rules to develop property in a certain way, yet the government denies the exercise of that right for 32 months and counting—but in the Court's view, forcing a decision (or compensation) would be unduly hasty or costly for the *government*. Still, the Court held out hope that in certain circumstances such delays could constitute a compensable temporary taking, noting that "the duration of the restriction is one of the important factors that a court must consider."[33]

Chief Justice Rehnquist dissented along with Justices Scalia and Thomas. The permit delays, he observed, actually had lasted six years, not the mere 32 months cited by the majority. Because "a ban on all development lasting almost six years does not resemble any traditional land-use planning device,"[34] and because during that period the ban amounted to a complete deprivation of the value of the property, the dissenters concluded the property owners were entitled to compensation. By refusing to compel fair and efficient land-use decisions, and by imposing on the hapless property owner the entire cost of bureaucratic delays, the Court created a perverse incentive for government officials to study and ponder endlessly without regard to property rights.

It may be true that in America a person's home is still his or her castle—but if so, the moat is filled with voracious alligators snapping at the castle owner's heels. This chapter barely skims the surface of the broad array of property rights deprivations visited upon Americans by their governments, encompassing not merely eminent domain abuse and regulatory takings, but laws regulating harmless consensual conduct within the home, asset forfeiture laws, and intrusive and excessive police searches.[35] Individual justices do not always consistently line up for property rights, instead rendering decisions seemingly on the basis of whose rights are being eviscerated.

Given that property rights are expressly protected in the Constitution—perhaps more than any other right—that they are in such jeopardy today seems odd. The Framers could not have known that the talents of future Supreme Court justices would extend from law to magic, possessed as they are of a remarkable ability to make written words vanish or to transform them into something altogether different from their original meaning. For that consequence we all suffer, but none more than those men and women who begin with few resources yet continue to aspire to the American Dream—a dream whose cornerstone is private property rights.

9. School Choice

Chue Yang is a 21-year-old junior at Georgetown University, majoring in history and English in preparation for a career as a college professor. Though her future is bright, she has had to come a long way. Chue emigrated to America with her family when she was in second grade. Neither Chue nor her parents knew any English. She enrolled in the Milwaukee Public Schools, which, at the time, were highly dysfunctional. Chue was forced to overcome not only her language barrier but substandard schooling.

By the time Chue reached middle school, she was able to obtain a half-tuition scholarship to attend a private school, where her circumstances improved. Her family found even half tuition difficult to afford, especially with three other children, but somehow they managed. As Chue recounts, "They saw that education was the only way out of poverty and to gain a better life."

When she was ready to start high school, Chue was offered an opportunity to advance her education and ease the burden on her parents at the same time. She received a publicly financed voucher through the Milwaukee Parental Choice Program, which is available to pay the full tuition of students in low-income families who wish to attend private schools. That program allowed Chue to attend Messmer High School, an independent Catholic school that serves an overwhelmingly minority and low-income (and largely non-Catholic) student population. The school's high standards and expectations and its philosophy of "no excuses" produce high graduation rates and impressive academic credentials. In Chue's case, the school equipped her for admission to one of the nation's top universities.

Today in Milwaukee, students may choose among a wide array of K–12 educational options, including public charter schools, private schools, and traditional public schools. The same is true for many students in Arizona, Ohio, Florida, Pennsylvania, and the nation's capital, which allow disadvantaged children to attend private schools using either vouchers or scholarships funded through tax

127

credits. Nationally, more than 100,000 disabled children in every state receive public support for private school tuition. More than that number receive vouchers for private preschools. And, of course, millions have received support through the G.I. Bill or Pell Grants to attend public or private postsecondary institutions.

In all of those settings, the educational marketplace is dynamic, characterized by widespread choice and competition. Children like Chue Yang and her siblings no longer are consigned to poor-performing government schools. Indeed, to attract students and the resources at their command, failing schools are forced to improve.

All of that seems quintessentially American. Yet to groups such as the American Civil Liberties Union and the perversely named People for the American Way—not to mention the powerful special-interest groups dedicated to preserving the educational status quo—school choice that includes religious schools is a violation of the separation of church and state.

As probably is apparent by now, I am not a fan of bar examinations. But if one is necessary, in my book the constitutional law section would consist of a single question: "Where in the Constitution is separation of church and state?" Any answer other than "nowhere" would indicate that the applicant does not possess the minimal reading skills or comprehension necessary to perform as an attorney. The whole doctrine of separation of church and state—embedded not only in American jurisprudence but also in the civics lessons absorbed by nearly all Americans—is an example of judicial activism that transforms the plain meaning of constitutional language.

That is not to deny that the Constitution's religion clauses mark a vitally important limitation on government power. Indeed, they create dual and complementary constraints. If one reads the actual language of the Constitution—an exercise all too uncommon in most law schools—one will find that the First Amendment states, "Congress shall make no law respecting an establishment of religion, or prohibiting the free exercise thereof." Hence, Congress (and later the states by operation of the Fourteenth Amendment) may neither establish religion nor prohibit its free exercise. As a fairly obvious rule of thumb, the government may not engage in religious indoctrination or coerce people to engage in religious practices (such as prayer in schools). But neither may government treat religion in a hostile or discriminatory manner. The Court of late seems to be grasping those lines of constitutional demarcation—but seemingly only because other rules have proven hopelessly subjective and impossible to apply fairly, clearly, or consistently.

The notion that allowing students to use state aid to attend the school of their choice—public, private, or religious—would constitute an "establishment of religion" would surely make the Framers' heads spin. Our nation has a tradition rich with religion. Yet the Framers also understood the danger of theocracy—not only to the rights of individuals, but also to the liberty of religious minorities. By forbidding "an establishment of religion" while protecting "the free exercise thereof," the Framers plainly were charting a course of governmental neutrality toward religion: government may not favor religion, but neither may it disfavor religion.[1] Moreover, in *Pierce v. Society of Sisters* and its progeny, the Supreme Court has interpreted the Constitution to reserve to parents the right to control their children's education; in *Brown v. Board of Education*, it established the sacred promise of equal educational opportunities for all schoolchildren (see chapter 4).

Given the plain language and obvious intent of the First Amendment religion clauses, and the broader constitutional context of parental liberty and equal educational opportunities, the constitutionality of school choice would seem like a no-brainer. Yet the battle to preserve school choice against federal constitutional challenges was far from easy, spanning a dozen cases over a 12-year period during which opponents won more rounds than supporters—and the ultimate triumph in the U.S. Supreme Court was by a single vote. Indeed, the saga of school-choice litigation is a case study of the risks and consequences of judicial interpretation untethered by the Constitution.[2]

The idea of school choice—that is, where government provides financial support for K–12 educational choices encompassing public, private, and religious schools—is credited to Thomas Paine and, in modern times, to the great economist and Nobel laureate Milton Friedman. School-choice programs first appeared in the late 1800s, when rural communities in Vermont and Maine decided not to construct their own public schools but instead to pay tuition for children to attend public or private schools of their choice.[3] In the 1970s, the widespread closure of religious schools led to the creation of "parochiaid" programs to help keep such schools afloat in states like Pennsylvania and New York. Around the same time, a handful of liberals, led by Berkeley law professor Jack Coons, began to call for school choice as a matter of social justice.

More recently, school choice has been aimed at expanding educational options for children in failing public schools, particularly low-income and minority schoolchildren. In 1990, the Milwaukee Parental Choice Program was enacted, giving several hundred low-income children control over their share of state education funds to pay tuition at nonsectarian private schools. (The program now provides vouchers for up to 22,500 children, and religious schools are among the options.) Subsequently, voucher programs were created in Cleveland, Ohio; Florida; and Washington, D.C., and programs providing tax credits for contributions to private scholarship programs have been enacted in Arizona, Florida, and Pennsylvania. School choice provides an educational life preserver for children who desperately need it, and the resulting competition encourages public schools to improve.[4]

But legal challenges to school-choice programs have become as inevitable as death and taxes, and often just as painful. The principal initial legal theory used by the unions and their allies was the First Amendment establishment clause. Although all of the legal challenges to date have been brought in state courts so the plaintiffs could use additional weapons found in state constitutions, the main goal of the anti-school-choice forces was to establish a national precedent under the establishment clause that would kill school choice in its infancy and across-the-board. There is something perverse in the spectacle of the teacher unions as guardians of the First Amendment. A visit to their website reveals nary a hint of concern about the values of the religion clauses, but a great deal of consternation about school choice. Great danger lurks in the hands of people for whom precious constitutional doctrines are but means to an end.

That school-choice opponents credibly could invoke the establishment clause was the result of decades of judicial activism, during which the Supreme Court transformed the First Amendment from a guarantee of neutrality toward religion into a doctrine of hostility toward religion. Establishment clause jurisprudence grew hopelessly complex and muddled. Government presumably may print the words "In God We Trust" on our coins and currency, and the

Supreme Court may begin its sessions with the words "God save this honorable Court," but nativity scenes can appear only in broader nonreligious contexts. Congress may begin its day with nonsectarian prayer but public schools may not. The constitutionality of direct aid to religious schools turns upon whether the government provides textbooks (permissible) or maps (forbidden), leading the late U.S. senator Danial Patrick Moynihan (D-NY) to quip, what about atlases, which are books of maps? Public school teachers could provide secular remedial instruction to religious school students, but only outside of religious school premises (leading to the widespread use of trailers outside many private schools). The confusion surrounding the establishment clause and the Court's seemingly arbitrary line-drawing has engendered constant, divisive litigation.

The Supreme Court first took up the question of aid to private schools and to the families who patronized them in 1973, when New York's and Pennsylvania's "parochiaid" programs were challenged under the First Amendment. The Court struck them down in a pair of decisions, the main one being *Committee for Public Education v. Nyquist*. Because the aid was restricted to private schools—most of which were religious—and to families patronizing them, the Court concluded that the "primary effect" of the aid programs was to advance religion. It mattered not at all that the support for private schools and their students amounted to a pittance compared with the subsidies of public schools, nor that the states would incur greater public school costs if the private schools were forced to close.

Fortunately, the Court held out some hope, reserving in a footnote the question of "whether the significantly religious character of the statute's beneficiaries might differentiate the present cases from a case involving some form of public assistance (e.g., scholarships) made available generally without regard to the sectarian-nonsectarian, or public-nonpublic nature of the institution benefitted."[5] In a word, neutrality. Over the 29 years after *Nyquist*, advocates (including me) worked to transform that narrow loophole into the governing constitutional principle.

The first opportunity was in a 1983 case, *Mueller v. Allen*, in which the Court considered the constitutionality of a Minnesota tax deduction for school expenses, including tuition.[6] The vast majority of people claiming deductions did so for payments to religious schools—after all, few public school parents incur direct educational

131

expenses, and most private schools are religiously affiliated. In a pathbreaking 5-4 decision by then-Justice William Rehnquist, the Court upheld the deductions. The program differed from *Nyquist*, the Court found, because the aid was transmitted to religious institutions only as the result of independent parental choices, and the range of options included both public and private schools. "The historic purposes of the [Establishment] Clause," Rehnquist explained, "simply do not encompass the sort of attenuated financial benefit, ultimately controlled by the private choices of individual parents, that eventually flows to parochial schools from the neutrally available tax benefit at issue in this case."[7] *Mueller* provided a congenial framework within which to design future school-choice programs.

In 1986, the Court unanimously upheld the use of college aid by a blind student, Larry Witters, studying for the ministry at a divinity school—about the most religious possible use of aid. But the Court's opinion, written by Justice Thurgood Marshall, emphasized that most of the religious institutions in which the aid could be used were nonsectarian and that relatively few students would use the aid for the purposes to which Witters had put it. If that was the governing principle, the battle for school choice in Witters's case might be won at the expense of the war, because a program's constitutionality might depend upon the number of students actually choosing to use the aid for religious purposes. How can the choices of third parties determine whether a statute is constitutional?

Fortunately, Justice Lewis Powell, who had authored the *Nyquist* decision, wrote a concurring opinion that went further than Marshall's opinion. Powell focused less on the numbers and more on the program's evenhandedness, declaring that "state programs that are wholly neutral in offering educational assistance to a class defined without reference to religion do not violate" the establishment clause.[8] In Witters's case, the class was disabled college students—would the same rule apply for a class of low-income schoolchildren in elementary and secondary schools? That question would hover menacingly over school-choice programs starting in 1995, when the Milwaukee program was expanded to include religious schools and the Cleveland and Arizona programs were created.

In 1993, the Court upheld 5-4 a program that provided a publicly funded interpreter for a deaf child in a Catholic high school.[9] The majority again applied the two *Mueller* criteria, neutrality and indi-rect aid. Notably, the interpreter's services included both secular and religious subjects, which meant that the Court was not drawing a bright-line distinction that would allow private schools to use aid provided through publicly financed scholarships only for secular instruction—a demand that most religious schools, which intertwine religious and secular instruction, could not satisfy.

Those were the precedents that existed when my colleagues and I at the Institute for Justice began defending school-choice programs against First Amendment challenges. We had the most-recent prece-dents on our side, but our opponents argued that *Nyquist* was more on point regarding the constitutionality of school-choice programs. Whether *Nyquist* or *Mueller* and its progeny would control the fate of countless children we would not know until the Court squarely decided the issue.

But the Court appeared in no rush to do so, possibly because neither of the two main factions on the Court was certain how Justice Sandra Day O'Connor would vote. She was usually the deciding and always the least-predictable justice in establishment clause cases. My colleagues and I won decisions upholding school-choice pro-grams against First Amendment challenges in the state supreme courts of Wisconsin,[10] Arizona,[11] and Ohio.[12] But the Supreme Court declined to review any of them, so school-choice programs continued to be at risk of a national precedent that could undo all of those victories in one fell swoop.

While we were litigating in state courts, the U.S. Supreme Court continued to dispense generally favorable jurisprudential tea leaves. In 1995, the Court ruled 5-4 that it was permissible for the University of Virginia to fund a religious publication as one of the numerous student activities for which the university provided financial sup-port. The "guarantee of neutrality," wrote Justice Anthony Kennedy for the majority, "is respected, not offended, when the government, following neutral criteria and evenhanded policies, extends benefits to recipients whose ideologies and viewpoints are broad and diverse."[13] Indeed, the Court ruled that excluding the religious publi-cation from otherwise generally available funding would constitute impermissible viewpoint discrimination.

The dissenters focused on the fact that the aid was direct. Previous cases upholding aid, Justice David Souter pointed out, "turned on the fact that the choice to benefit religion was made by a non-religious third party standing between the government and a religious institution."[14] In that regard, the dissent gave us hope, because school-choice programs not only were neutral toward religion but also involved the transmission of public funds by independent third parties, namely parents.

Two years later, the same 5-4 majority took the neutrality rule another step forward. In *Agostini v. Felton*, the Court overturned past precedents to allow the use of public school teachers to provide remedial instruction to religious school students on religious school premises. To us, *Agostini* presented a tougher case than school choice, because it involved public school employees teaching in religious schools at government expense. Such a relationship might raise concerns of symbolism—the commingling of church and state—that had troubled several justices, including Justice Sandra Day O'Connor, in other contexts. By contrast, school choice involved indirect aid that would create no visible perception of religious "endorsement."

Still, the Court upheld the aid. In the process, it adjusted ever so slightly—but significantly—its definition of neutrality. Aid programs, the Court declared, do not offend the establishment clause "where the aid is allocated on the basis of neutral, secular criteria that neither favor nor disfavor religion, and is made available to both religious and secular beneficiaries on a nondiscriminatory basis."[15] In prior cases, the Court had defined neutrality as evenhandedness between public and private entities. Here, the Court suggested neutrality meant nondiscrimination between religious and nonreligious providers. In other words, a school-choice program need not necessarily encompass public school options in order to pass constitutional muster.

Unfortunately, the penultimate decision before the Supreme Court tackled the school-choice issue muddied the waters. In *Mitchell v. Helms*,[16] the Court in 2000 upheld direct aid to private and religious schools in the form of computers and other equipment. The good news was that the decision was 6-3, with Justice Stephen Breyer supporting the result. What was troubling was that Justices O'Connor and Breyer paired together in a separate decision. While the plurality decision by Justice Clarence Thomas emphasized neutrality, O'Connor and Breyer stated that in the case of "direct aid" (as opposed to "indirect aid," which was characterized by "true private-choice"), it was important that no government funds would reach the coffers of religious schools. How funds used to purchase computers that are provided to religious schools pose any lesser threat of establishing religion than funds provided to religious schools to purchase computers themselves is not clear (perhaps the extra layer of bureaucracy and inefficiency attenuates the taint). But it introduced new uncertainty into the equation even as the neutral aid was approved.

Because the deciding duo continued to embrace the distinction between direct and indirect aid even as they found neutrality alone insufficient, the decision itself did not sound alarm bells. Our opponents, however, quickly seized on the language about no funds reaching religious school coffers. And my colleagues and I worried about the possible influence of Justice Breyer on Justice O'Connor, which we perceived as anything but beneficent.

The case that finally reached the Supreme Court involved the Cleveland school-choice program, which had been upheld against a First Amendment challenge by the Ohio Supreme Court but struck down by the U.S. Court of Appeals for the Sixth Circuit. The case presented both favorable and unfavorable facts. On the one hand, the Cleveland Public Schools were abysmal. A child in the public schools had a slightly less than 1 in 14 chance of graduating on time with senior-level proficiency—and a slightly greater than 1 in 14 chance of being a victim of crime inside the schools each year. On the other hand, roughly 97 percent of the children in the program attended religious schools. Suburban public schools had been invited to participate, but all had refused. Cleveland schoolchildren had choices that included public charter and magnet schools, but they predated the private school-choice program. So the Court's definition of "neutrality" might very well determine the program's constitutionality.

Though we were worried about Justice O'Connor's vote, she came through, writing a concurring opinion but embracing the masterful 5-4 majority opinion by Chief Justice Rehnquist. The Court ruled in *Zelman v. Simmons-Harris* that "where a government aid program is neutral with respect to religion, and provides assistance to a broad class of citizens who, in turn, direct government aid to religious schools wholly as a result of their own genuine and independent private choice, it is not readily subject to challenge under the Establishment Clause."[17] It was the Super Bowl for school choice—and the kids won.

In a poignant concurring opinion, Justice Thomas found that the Cleveland program "does not force any individual to submit to religious indoctrination or education. It simply gives parents a greater choice as to where and in what manner to educate their children."[18] As usual, he examined the history of the establishment clause, and he found no evidence of intent to bar neutral government assistance. Moreover, he noted that the First Amendment had been applied to the states through the Fourteenth Amendment, whose goal was to "advance, not constrain, individual liberty." There would be a "tragic irony in converting the Fourteenth Amendment from a guarantee of opportunity to an obstacle against education reform,"[19] Thomas declared, which would leave intact a status quo "that distorts our constitutional values and disserves those in the greatest need."[20]

The dissents were strident, hyperbolic, and hysterical. Justice Stevens raised the specter of "religious strife" of the type seen in "the Balkans, Northern Ireland, and the Middle East"[21]—concerns echoed by Justice Souter's claims of "divisiveness"[22] and Justice Breyer's warnings of "religiously based social conflict."[23] The majority aptly dismissed those concerns, quipping that "the program has ignited no 'divisiveness' or 'strife' other than this litigation."[24] Indeed, in Milwaukee, Cleveland, Florida, and our nation's capital, all of which have school voucher programs, we see no religious jihads or marches in the streets; we do see children who previously were consigned to educational cesspools now learning in safe and nurturing educational environments chosen by their parents. The school-choice phenomenon seems clearly not a violation but a vindication of our constitutional principles.

Justice Breyer's vote in *Zelman*, as I have previously observed, was deeply disappointing. The enactment of school-choice programs would seem to reflect the ultimate expression of "active liberty" that Breyer believes animates the Constitution. Moreover, school-choice programs readily satisfy the framework he articulated in his concurring opinion in *Mitchell*. But fortunately, the majority of the Court (though by the barest of margins) faithfully applied constitutional intent, and American schoolchildren are the fortunate beneficiaries.

But the voucher wars are far from over. Although the federal constitutionality of school choice is firmly established, the battleground has shifted to the states. Several dozen states have Blaine amendments in their own constitutions, which typically prohibit aid for the "benefit" or "support" of churches or sectarian schools. The First Amendment, too, prohibits aid for the support or benefit of religion. School choice, by contrast, provides aid for the support and benefit of students. Indeed, the Wisconsin and Arizona Supreme Courts upheld school-choice programs against Blaine amendment challenges.[25]

The Blaine amendments are a relic of the nativist movement of the late 19th century. Nativists exploited fears about Catholic immigrants and the schools they brought with them to preserve Protestant hegemony over public schools and to promote a federal constitutional amendment to ban aid to "sectarian" (that is, Catholic) schools. The amendment failed, but it was followed by dozens of successful attempts to graft similar language onto state constitutions, often as a condition of admission of states into the Union.[26] In his plurality opinion in *Mitchell*, Justice Thomas, along with Chief Justice Rehnquist and Justices Kennedy and Scalia, remarked that "hostility to aid to pervasively sectarian schools has a shameful pedigree that we do not hesitate to disavow." He added: "[N]othing in the Establishment Clause requires the exclusion of pervasively sectarian schools from otherwise permissible aid programs, and other doctrines of this Court bar it. This doctrine, born of bigotry, should be buried now."[27]

Were a state court to construe a Blaine amendment to forbid the inclusion of religious schools in a choice program, it would constitute discrimination against religion in violation of the guarantee of neutrality toward religion as articulated in such cases as the University of Virginia decision and *Agostini*. Such was the case when Washington state, adhering to a broad application of its Blaine amendment, singled out students studying for the divinity from a postsecondary grant program available to all other students.

School-choice advocates hoped that the Supreme Court would put an end to discriminatory applications of the Blaine amendments. But once again, the principled fervor of the Rehnquist Court waned. In a disappointing 6-3 ruling in *Locke v. Davey*,[28] the Court upheld Washington state's exclusion of divinity students from the grant program. Assigning the decision to himself,[29] Chief Justice Rehnquist wrote an extremely narrow opinion emphasizing the long tradition of states' denying direct financial assistance to ministers. The Court left open the possibility of a challenge to discrimination against religious options in other contexts.

That such cases will have to be fought, unfortunately, is a certainty. At a debate in New York I had with the National Education Association's Robert Chanin around the time of the *Zelman* decision, my longtime legal nemesis referred to the well-equipped legal "toolbox" available to school-choice opponents, containing all manner of "Mickey Mouse provisions" found in state constitutions. I resented that comment: after all, Mickey Mouse loves children. But the underlying message was sobering, indicating that even after our victory in the U.S. Supreme Court, school-choice advocates would have to continue to fight a war of attrition every step of the way. And indeed, following the triumph in the U.S. Supreme Court, the Colorado and Florida Supreme Courts struck down school-choice programs under precisely the types of state constitutional provisions that Chanin warned about, thereby denying precious educational opportunities to thousands of schoolchildren who needed them desperately.[30]

Fortunately, more often than not, freedom prevails in the courts. The *Zelman* decision is a shining example of the judiciary's interpreting the Constitution in fidelity with its intended meaning. In the process, all Americans ultimately will prosper from the freedom the Court so wisely preserved.

But the battle goes on. As long as some judges are willing to do the bidding of special-interest groups and distort the rule of law, those groups will continue to wield constitutions to stifle the very freedoms they were designed to protect. If the special interests succeed, too few children will be able to follow in Chue Yang's footsteps toward a brighter educational future.

10. State Constitutions: The Beckoning Frontier

Randy Bailey is a bear of a guy. The hard-working family man owns Bailey's Brake Service at the corner of Main and Country Club in Mesa, Arizona, where scores of customers have had their brakes expertly serviced and repaired for more than 20 years. Randy bought the business from his father and hopes to pass it down to his son someday. He is honest, takes care of his property, pays taxes, provides employment to other men, and bothers nobody.

All of which, of course, makes him a juicy target for voracious city bureaucrats.

In the 1990s, Ken Lenhart, who owns an Ace Hardware store, decided he wanted to expand. The location he coveted was at the corner of Country Club and Main, one of Mesa's prime intersections. The property was occupied by several homes and small businesses, including Bailey's Brake Service.

Lenhart began purchasing some of the property, which he allowed to deteriorate. But instead of trying to purchase the rest, he went to the city, demanding that Mesa obtain the remaining parcels and transfer ownership to him. Driving an all-too-familiar bargain, Mesa officials agreed to do exactly that, but only if Lenhart would accept a $2 million subsidy as well.

Mesa added the property to a preexisting redevelopment zone, where the planners wanted a "gateway" to the city. What better gateway than a hardware store? The city crafted development specifications that, remarkably, called for a project precisely along the lines that Lenhart wanted to build. Equally remarkable, Lenhart won the bid.

Randy Bailey had no objection to the project, as long as he could be a part of it. He contacted Lenhart and offered to move his building to another location on the same corner if it would be more convenient. Lenhart told him to talk to the city. When Randy called city officials, they told him they indeed wanted him to move, but somewhere else altogether. There would be no room for Bailey's Brake Service at Country Club and Main. They were taking his property.

Mesa followed most of the technical requirements, if not the spirit, of Arizona's redevelopment statute, which allows takings to remove blight. The redevelopment plan purported to redress a housing shortage in Mesa—although its effect would be to bulldoze houses while replacing none. And much of the "blight" identified by the city was on property owned by Lenhart.

After Bailey raised a fuss, the city offered to move his business to a less-desirable location and continuously increased its compensation offer. Bailey was just greedy, city officials contended. They simply could not fathom the concept that Bailey did not want to move, no matter how high the price.

At first glance, Randy Bailey's circumstances seemed to resemble Susette Kelo's in Connecticut. As recounted in chapter 8, Kelo's efforts under the federal constitution to protect her property were unavailing.

But Randy had a resource at his disposal that Susette Kelo did not: a nifty provision of the Arizona Constitution that says "[p]rivate property shall not be taken for private use." After listing specific exceptions, the provision goes on to state that "[w]henever an attempt is made to take private property for a use alleged to be public, the question whether the contemplated use be really public shall be a judicial question, and determined as such without regard to any legislative assertion that the use is public."

Still, my Institute for Justice colleague Timothy Keller and I faced an uphill battle to protect Randy's property. The state courts had issued a series of decisions suggesting that a showing of "public benefit" might suffice for a taking, and the state's redevelopment statutes watered down the standard even more. Relying on those authorities, the trial court upheld the city's use of eminent domain.

But in a landmark ruling, the Arizona Court of Appeals reversed the decision. The city had cited federal precedents in support of its arguments, but the court rejected them. "The federal constitution provides considerably less protection against eminent domain than our Constitution provides," the court explained, and thus federal cases provide little assistance in interpreting the Arizona provision.[1]

The court ruled that "if the government proposes to take property and then convey it to private developers for private commercial use, a significant question is presented because of the intended disposition of the property."[2] It held that the "constitutional requirement of 'public use' is satisfied only when the public benefits and characteristics of the intended use substantially predominate over the private nature of that use."[3] Applying a list of factors, the court concluded that the attempted taking of Bailey's property was for private rather than public use and therefore fell outside the city's authority.

Public sentiment, fueled by extensive local media coverage and a *60 Minutes* segment, led both the city (through voter initiative) and the state to tighten restrictions on eminent domain. Happily, Randy Bailey still sells brakes at the corner of Main and Country Club.

The Arizona decision is not the only instance in which state courts have interpreted their own constitutions to provide greater protection against eminent domain abuse than the federal constitution. In Michigan, the state supreme court in 1981 issued an infamous decision in *Poletown Neighborhood Council v. City of Detroit*, upholding the use of eminent domain to make way for a General Motors factory. "The power of eminent domain is to be used in this instance primarily to accomplish the essential public purposes of alleviating unemployment and revitalizing the economic base of the community," the court declared. "The benefit to a private interest is merely incidental."[4] In a classic example of the disastrous consequences of government planning, the plant was never built, though in the aborted process much of the community it was supposed to revitalize was destroyed.[5]

But in 2004, the current Michigan Supreme Court—one of the finest in the nation—voted to overrule *Poletown*. The case involved a similar grandiose scheme to redevelop an area outside of the Wayne County airport by taking private land and transferring it to developers to build a business and technology park.

In an opinion by Justice Robert P. Young Jr., the court found that the county's plan satisfied the state's redevelopment statute because it unquestionably would "benefit the public" through job creation, tax revenues, and so on.[6] But whether the county's exercise of its statutory powers was constitutional was a different question. Unlike in Arizona, the court did not have before it a broadly worded state constitutional provision; indeed, the wording of its public use clause is virtually identical to that of the Fifth Amendment. So how could the Michigan Supreme Court reach a decision construing nearly identical language to require an actual public use rather than a mere public benefit when the U.S. Supreme Court has failed to do so?

Simple: state courts are not bound to interpret their *own* constitutions in lockstep with the U.S. Supreme Court, even if the language of the provisions is identical. One of the sweetest fruits of our system of federalism is that the U.S. Constitution provides only the *floor* beneath which the protection of liberty may not descend. But state courts are free to go beyond federal constitutional protections (or, more to the point, beyond protections recognized by federal courts) in construing their own state constitutions.

And that is exactly what the Michigan Supreme Court did in its *Wayne County* decision. The explanation for the divergence with the *Kelo* decision is that the Michigan Supreme Court applied the plain meaning and original intent of the public use limitation, whereas the U.S. Supreme Court did not. The Michigan court recited that the "primary objective in interpreting a constitutional provision is to determine the text's original meaning to the ratifiers, the people, at the time of ratification."[7] The court traced Michigan jurisprudence at the time that the state constitution was ratified in 1963. At the time, although property could be taken and transferred to private parties for public use, it was clear that "the constitutional 'public use' requirement worked to prohibit the state from transferring condemned property to private entities for a *private* use."[8] Indeed, the court before that time never had held that a public use is established "simply because one entity's profit maximization contributed to the health of the general economy."[9]

Unlike the U.S. Supreme Court, the Michigan Supreme Court did not perceive that the meaning of the public use provision somehow had been amended since its adoption, and because its prior decision in *Poletown* was "a radical and unabashed departure" from the original understanding, the decision could no longer be given the force of law.[10] Moreover, unlike slum clearance cases, "the only public benefits . . . arise after the lands are acquired by the government and put to private use." Thus, the taking was unconstitutional.[11]

For those who may despair over the state of our liberties under the national Constitution, then, some hope exists that thanks to federalism, pockets of liberty still prosper around the nation. Property rights may be suspended in many places, but apparently they are alive and well in Arizona, Michigan, and elsewhere.

The question for freedom activists is how can we make those pockets of freedom bigger?

The Untapped Potential of State Constitutions

One of the few characteristics unifying conservatives and libertarians (along with many liberals) is that nearly all of us extol the virtues of federalism. It is therefore ironic that since conservative and libertarian public interest litigation began in earnest in the late 1970s, the overwhelming majority of cases have skirted state constitutional issues and focused instead on vindicating federal constitutional guarantees in federal courts. In a certain sense, such an emphasis is understandable. Federal cases have broader precedential value. And it would be a shame not to seize opportunities presented by the appointment of federal justices and judges who understand and generally adhere to a philosophy of original intent.

But important as that continuing federal litigation campaign is, a strategy focused primarily on federal constitutional litigation has serious shortcomings, and those shortcomings are abundantly apparent in the preceding pages. Were our national Constitution interpreted to provide a general rule of liberty to which permissible uses of government power were the exception, little recourse to state courts would be necessary. But we are quite far from that understanding today. Although prospects seem to exist for further revival of abandoned federal constitutional liberties, in general the courts have been very reluctant to overturn their own precedents, even when they are clearly contrary to plain meaning and original intent. The evolution of the Rehnquist Court illustrates how quickly a judicial counterrevolution can lose its energy. Whether the momentum toward greater liberty will resume afresh in the Roberts Court is an open question. To be sure, the freedom movement needs to be vigilant in protecting federal constitutional liberties regardless of whether it still can press forward. But the next frontier for the freedom movement ought to be the vindication of constitutional liberties in *state* constitutions.

One legitimately might ask, given the slow progress we have witnessed in expanding liberty through federal litigation, how the freedom movement possibly could expect greater results by spreading its limited resources among 50 state constitutions. The first two parts of the answer are illustrated by the Arizona and Michigan eminent domain cases discussed earlier in this chapter. First, state constitutions often contain far more numerous and explicit limitations on government power than the national Constitution. State constitutions that were created in the founding era, as well as states created from the Northwest Ordinance, were particularly influenced by natural rights philosophy. Likewise, state constitutions adopted during the Progressive era reflected cynicism about the power of representative government, particularly when beholden to special interests, and they contain abundant limits on the exercise of government power. Many of those limits are dormant, not because they have been read out of the constitution but because no one asserts them in constitutional litigation. Other limitations are quite vibrant but often are not adroitly applied to protect liberty.

Second, as noted, state courts are free to establish greater protections for liberty than those recognized by their national counterparts. Conservatives and libertarians should argue forcefully for an independent interpretation of state constitutional provisions by state courts, in accord with plain meaning and original intent.

An additional reason for pursuing state constitutional litigation is that although no state court decision is binding in other states, courts in one state often look to courts in other states for guidance in interpreting similar constitutional language. Many of the restraints on government power are found in multiple state constitutions, so winning a favorable decision in one state court can create precedential effect in other states.

But the main reason to pursue state constitutional litigation is that our nation's Framers intended that state constitutions would provide the first line of defense for our liberties. As Washington Supreme Court Justice Richard Sanders has observed: "The Bill of Rights, at most, was to be but a second layer of protection. The state declarations of rights, on the other hand, were meant to be the primary source of protection."[12]

Those of us who believe in original intent ought to vindicate the Founders' genius through recourse to state constitutional protections. State constitutions largely are virgin territory for the freedom movement. Given the erosion of liberty that we are experiencing at the hands of every level of government, nothing could be clearer than that we should use every tool at our disposal to protect our freedom. The potential of state constitutions is enormous and almost completely untapped.

144

As is so often the case, the left has done much of the legal trailblazing. The architect of the left's remarkable state constitutional litigation efforts was U.S. Supreme Court Justice William Brennan, whose call to action came in the form of a pair of seminal law review articles in 1977 and 1986. Brennan had enjoyed a good run as the intellectual godfather of the Warren Court, but with the emergence of a more conservative federal judiciary that began construing constitutional guarantees more narrowly starting in the 1970s, he could read the writing on the wall. And he had a plan.

Although hardly an apostle of the Tenth Amendment, Brennan become an enthusiast for federalism in one important respect: he extolled the virtue of state courts' reading guarantees of state constitutions more broadly than the national constitution. Though his articles were a clarion call to liberal activists, his message ought to resonate just as strongly—if not more so—among conservatives and libertarians. As Brennan proclaimed:

> the point I want to stress here is that state courts cannot rest when they have afforded their citizens the full protections of the federal Constitution. State constitutions, too, are a font of individual liberties, their protections often extending beyond those required by the Supreme Court's interpretation of federal law. The legal revolution which has brought federal law to the fore must not be allowed to inhibit the independent protective force of state law—for without it, the full realization of our liberties cannot be guaranteed.[13]

Brennan cited Madison's warning that state governments could pose a greater threat to liberty than the national government. In fact, Madison had proposed explicit constraints on state power within the Bill of Rights. But his suggestion was defeated, according to Brennan, because "it was believed that personal freedom could be secured more accurately by decentralization than by express command." In other words, "the states were perceived as protectors of, rather than threats to, the civil and political rights of individuals."[14] Though Madison's views subsequently prevailed through the adoption of the Fourteenth Amendment, state courts retain the power to interpret state constitutional rights more broadly than federal constitutional rights. "As is well known, federal preservation of civil liberties is a minimum, which the states may surpass so long as there is no clash with federal law." In light of the perceived retrenchment in the interpretation of federal constitutional rights, Brennan called upon state courts to move the ball forward, and they did exactly that. Indeed, by 1984, Brennan counted "over 250 published opinions holding that constitutional minimums set by the United States Supreme Court were insufficient to satisfy the more stringent requirements of state constitutional law."[15]

Remarked Brennan, "Every believer in our concept of federalism, and I am a devout believer, must salute this development in our state courts."[16] He argued that "those who regard judicial review as inconsistent with our democratic system—a view I do not share—should find constitutional interpretation by the state judiciary less objectionable than activist intervention by their federal counterparts."[17] In addition to the Framers' intent that state constitutions would play a protective role in securing liberties, Brennan noted that many state judges themselves are subject to democratic processes and that state constitutions typically are more easily amended than the national constitution.

"This rebirth of interest in state constitutional law should be greeted with equal enthusiasm by all those who support our federal system, liberals and conservatives alike," Brennan observed, though he quipped tellingly that "[a]s state courts assume a leadership role in the protection of individual rights and liberties, the true colors of purported federalists will be revealed."[18] Surely somewhere in the heavens Brennan is smiling over the spectacle of social conservatives rushing to amend the national constitution to overturn state court decisions interpreting their constitutions to establish a right for homosexuals to marry.

Although the left has enjoyed substantial success through state constitutional litigation—after all, as my Alliance for School Choice colleague Scott Jensen observes, you need to be present to win—I suspect that conservatives and libertarians could do even better if they chose to systematically engage in the enterprise of shaping state constitutional jurisprudence. That is because so many of the provisions in state constitutions are aimed at *restricting* government power. A survey of state constitutions yields a number of provisions that could be wielded by freedom advocates. Many of those provisions have no counterparts in the federal constitution—and where they do, it is important always to keep in mind that federal constitutional protection only provides the *starting point* for state constitutional interpretation. In addition to public use provisions that are found in most state constitutions, promising doctrines and provisions found in multiple state constitutions include the following:

- *Taxpayer standing*. In federal courts, taxpayers usually do not have standing. A plaintiff raising federal constitutional claims must assert a particularized injury—one that is not shared in equal measure by all citizens. As a result, in many cases, such as excessive government spending, *no one* has standing to challenge unconstitutional government actions. By contrast, in state courts, taxpayers generally have standing to challenge almost any exercise of government power. That is why, for example, one sees challenges of municipally funded sports stadiums or other government boondoggles (no editorial insinuation intended, of course) in state courts, whereas similar federal government projects typically are unchallengeable.
- *Municipal* ultra vires. Here's a Latin phrase worth knowing. The federal government and many state governments generally are considered omnipotent, so that courts will uphold exercises of their power unless constrained by specific constitutional limitations. Under most state constitutions, however, municipal governments (including cities, school boards, and other local entities) possess only such powers as are expressly conferred by the state constitution or statute. Hence, taxpayers may challenge municipal power not only under specific constitutional limitations but also on the ground that the power exceeds the entity's corporate powers. That is, of course, the way constitutional review of *all* government power ought to be conducted, but at least it still exists with regard to municipal power, which all too frequently is abused.
- *General liberty provisions*. A number of state constitutions, especially the older ones, begin with statements of general principles that resemble the Declaration of Independence, particularly in their explicit protections of life, liberty, the pursuit of happiness, and property. Article I of the Washington Constitution, for instance, declares, "All political power is inherent in the people, and governments derive their just powers from the consent

of the governed, and are established to protect and maintain individual rights." Section 2 of Kentucky's Bill of Rights and Wyoming Constitution, article I, section 7, provide, "Absolute and arbitrary power over the lives, liberty and property of freemen exists nowhere in a republic, not even in the largest majority." At the very least, such provisions can be argued as background principles that create a presumption in favor of liberty.

- *Right of free labor*. Several state constitutions explicitly protect the freedom to pursue a livelihood, which provides greater textual support for economic liberty than the U.S. Constitution. Article I, section 1 of the Alaska Constitution, for example, states that "[t]his constitution is dedicated to the principles that all persons have a natural right to life, liberty, and the pursuit of happiness, and the enjoyment of the rewards of their own industry." Similarly, many constitutions safeguard the privileges and immunities of citizens, which state courts are free to interpret more expansively than the federal courts with regard to protecting economic liberty. Several state courts also have interpreted their due process and equal protection clauses to protect economic liberty.

- *Anti-monopoly provisions*. Closely related are express prohibitions of government monopolies contained in several constitutions. Article I, section 34, of the North Carolina Constitution is typical in providing, "Perpetuities and monopolies are contrary to the genius of a free state and shall not be allowed." Such provisions could be applied to prevent government from conferring exclusive monopolies or creating barriers to entry into businesses and professions, while not foreclosing market power legitimately garnered by competitors without government assistance.

- *Contract clauses*. Most state constitutions prohibit interference with contracts. Those prohibitions could be applied more expansively than their federal counterpart to constrain economic regulations.

- *Anti-forfeiture provisions*. Many state constitutions contain provisions forbidding forfeiture of estates in criminal cases, excessive fines, and cruel and unusual punishment. Such provisions, along with due process guarantees, could be wielded against abusive government civil asset forfeiture practices, as well as to limit excessive awards in tort cases.

- *Gift clauses.* Several state constitutions prohibit government from providing gifts. Such provisions could be used to prevent various types of corporate welfare, especially direct subsidies.
- *Private or local bill clauses.* State constitutions often prohibit state legislatures from conferring benefits upon a specific private or local interest that is not enacted as separate, standalone legislation. Such provisions are designed to prevent "log-rolling" and pork-barrel spending (if only the national Constitution contained such a provision!). Budget bills containing all manner of new programs that were not subjected to separate legislative votes are prime targets for such provisions.
- *Tax and borrowing restrictions.* Many constitutions limit government taxation and borrowing. Sophisticated taxpayer organizations could back up their fiscal analyses with litigation to enforce constitutional constraints against governmental entities that play fast and loose with the rules.
- *Victims' rights.* Criminal law ordinarily pits the defendant against the state, as if the crime was committed against society rather than against the victim. The process provides no formal standing to the victim, no matter how aggrieved. As a result of legal reforms, over half of state constitutions now provide constitutional protections to crime victims, such as the right to participate in sentencing decisions, the right to be informed about parole hearings, and the right to restitution. Several groups now are seeking to enforce those rights by providing independent legal representation to victims in criminal prosecutions.[19]

Such provisions barely scratch the surface of the many structural limits on government power and substantive protections of individual rights to be found in state constitutions. Several pro-freedom organizations, such as the Institute for Justice, Pacific Legal Foundation, North Carolina Institute for Constitutional Law, and Oregonians in Action are actively defending liberty under state constitutions. But far more such efforts are necessary, particularly indigenous state-based efforts in which lawyers can master the intricacies of state constitutions and apply them toward their intended ends.

That project raises questions regarding the philosophy and competence of state judges. As in the litigation context, conservative and libertarian activists have concentrated with regard to appointments on the federal judiciary, often ignoring state judiciaries. That strategy can come back to haunt them when state courts engage in judicial lawlessness, which if predicated on independent state constitutional grounds cannot be challenged in a federal judicial forum.[20]

The quality of state judges varies widely. Many are conscientious and have great integrity. Many others are political hacks. Only a few are steeped in the intricacies of state constitutional law, making all the more vital that advocates come well prepared. In many states, judges are elected; in others, advocates can influence judicial selection in other ways. Freedom advocates should devote much greater attention to this vital arena, urging the appointment of judges who will take seriously their role in safeguarding liberties protected by state constitutions.

Exemplars of State Constitutionalism

State court judges often toil in obscurity, but a large number have made their mark. Several liberal state supreme court justices, such as retired Arizona Supreme Court justice Stanley Feldman and Wisconsin chief justice Shirley Abrahamson, heeded Justice Brennan's call for state constitutional activism and blazed new legal trails in their states. Historically, state judges such as the revered U.S. senator Sam Ervin (D-NC), who served as a justice of the North Carolina Supreme Court from 1948 to 1954, vigorously applied state constitutional protections to individual liberty. More recently, other state court judges have begun developing state constitutional jurisprudence to vindicate the libertarian design of American federalism.

Two justices in particular provide excellent examples of that trend: Washington Supreme Court justice Richard Sanders and former California Supreme Court justice Janice Rogers Brown (who now serves as a judge on the U.S. Court of Appeals for the District of Columbia Circuit). They are exemplary for several reasons. Both are students of their state constitutions and advocates of independent state constitutional review. Both faithfully interpret their constitutions in accordance with plain meaning and original intent. And both consistently read state constitutional protections broadly, regardless of whether the liberty is invoked by a property owner or a criminal defendant.

As a result, they illustrate well the jurisprudence that can result from a vigorous interpretation of state constitutions in accord with their original intent.

Many of Justice Sanders's best opinions are dissents, unfortunately, but his powerful vision of the state constitution has moved the Washington Supreme Court in a more libertarian direction on such issues as economic liberty and religious freedom. In one case, Justice Sanders helped bring the court back from the precipice of interpreting Washington's Blaine amendment, which forbids state funding for religious purposes, in a manner that exhibits hostility toward religion. At issue was a voluntary chaplaincy program in a sheriff's office. In upholding the program, Justice Sanders noted that the Washington Constitution and its federal counterpart "both affirm the individual's right to free exercise while (or by) denouncing governmental involvement as a means to that end." But such clauses are "complementary, not contradictory," for both "promote . . . religious freedom."[21]

In conducting an independent analysis of the state constitutional provisions, Sanders observed that "[a]ppropriate constitutional analysis begins with the text and, for most purposes, should end there as well." The court's "objective is to define the constitutional principle in accordance with the original understanding of the ratifying public so as to faithfully apply the principle to each situation which might thereafter arise."[22] In this case, the analysis was straightforward: the constitution prohibits appropriations, none of which were made because the chaplain was an uncompensated volunteer. The plaintiff taxpayer "has simply not been compelled to furnish contributions of money to propagate opinions with which he disagrees," so there was no constitutional violation.[23]

A few years later, Justice Sanders found himself in dissent in a case construing the religious liberty guarantee of the state constitution in which the court upheld a zoning ordinance requiring churches to obtain a conditional use permit in order to operate. The court examined the ordinance under both the First Amendment and the Washington Constitution.

For Sanders, the law was problematic for two reasons. First, it imposed a bureaucratic obstacle to the free exercise of religion. Second, it vested unbridled discretion in local officials. Because freedom of religion under the Washington Constitution is "absolute," Sanders argued that the burden of persuasion rested with the county. And because there was no showing that the county's objectives could not be satisfied by neutral, less-restrictive regulations, the ordinance was "blatantly unconstitutional."[24]

Sanders urged his colleagues to "examine the facts before us, and measure them against the timeless principles and mandatory standard our constitution has provided." Although the otherwise absolute language was tempered by specific limited exceptions, there "is no zoning law exception to that constitutional guarantee of religious freedom so clearly incorporated in our constitutional text."[25] The majority had concluded that the state's and its subdivisions' inherent regulatory powers trumped the constitutional guarantee. Sanders declared, "I disagree: if religious liberty, or any civil liberty for that matter, is at the mercy of the police power, it is no civil liberty at all."[26]

Justice Sanders also dissented from a decision striking down an initiative creating legislative term limits. Turning to the plain language of the relevant constitutional provision that set qualifications for legislative officeholders, Sanders charged that the "majority errs when it concludes negative constitutional language which sets a minimum exclusively sets a maximum as well."[27] Other state constitutions used exclusive language, but the framers of the Washington Constitution did not. Such restrictions on legislative tenure were consistent not only with plain meaning, original intent, subsequent legislative practice, and the interpretation of similar language in other states, but also with the "spirit of our constitution," whose "very nature" is "to limit government." As Sanders explained, "Term limits, which ensure our legislators remain citizen legislators, not career state employees, are generally consistent with this constitutional framework and specifically consistent with our citizens' historically populist mistrust of the legislature."[28]

In *State of Washington v. Ladson*, the court examined the use of "pretextual stops" by police officers—that is, where a motorist is stopped for a minor traffic offense so that the police can look for evidence of more serious crimes. In this case, officers recognized the defendant as a reputed drug dealer and stopped him on the ground that his license tags had expired five days earlier. Then they discovered his driver's license was suspended and arrested him. A search revealed a handgun, several bags of marijuana, and $600 in cash.

The U.S. Supreme Court had sanctioned such stops, but in a majority opinion by Justice Sanders, the Washington Supreme Court determined such stops were forbidden by the state constitution. The Washington Constitution provides, "No person shall be disturbed in his private affairs, or his home invaded, without authority of law." Finding that the state constitutional proscription was broader than its federal counterpart, Sanders concluded that it "forbids use of pretext as a justification for a warrantless search or seizure because [it] requires that we look behind the formal justification for the stop to the actual one."[29]

In a 2004 decision, the Washington Supreme Court upheld an ordinance forbidding the posting of signs on public utility poles. Dissenting, Justice Sanders noted the sweeping nature of the state constitution's free-speech guarantee, noting that "today's majority denies [the defendant] the right to speak, write, and publish in a manner utilized since statehood."[30] The majority blindly followed federal precedent, ignoring the fact that under Washington state law, public utility poles are public forums, on which speech may be regulated in a reasonable and nondiscriminatory manner but not prohibited. "Regardless of what previously transpired in federal First Amendment litigation," Sanders urged, "it cannot rob our state constitution of its independent life and vitality."[31]

Two states to the south, Justice Janice Rogers Brown, who served on the California Supreme Court from 1996 to 2005, worked to broadly construe the state constitution's protected liberties and limits on government power. In *Aguilar v. Avis Rent a Car System*, the California Supreme Court upheld an injunction forbidding an employee from using racial epithets in the workplace. Justice Brown dissented, noting that the California Constitution provides: "Every person may freely speak, publish and write his or her sentiments on all subjects, being responsible for the abuse of this right. A law may not restrain or abridge liberty of speech or press." The provision clearly forbids prior restraint on speech, Brown reasoned. "In permitting speech, but requiring the speaker to pay damages for injurious speech, the California Constitution preserves both the freedom of the speaker and the equal dignity of the audience."[32]

In a rhetorical flourish that characterizes Justice Brown's writing, she underscored the vital principles underlying the constitutional protection. Acknowledging the speech at issue as "offensive and abhorrent," Brown observed: "[o]ne of the truths we hold to be self-evident is that a government that tells its citizens what they may *say* will soon be dictating what they may *think*. . . . I can conceive no imprisonment so complete, no subjugation so absolute, no abasement so abject as the enslavement of the mind."[33]

Writing for the court in the first case applying Proposition 209, the state constitutional amendment that banned racial preferences in government employment, education, and contracting, Justice Brown found that the provision's plain language and intent prohibited a local government minority subcontractor set-aside program. Moreover, Brown noted that although the federal constitution as construed by the U.S. Supreme Court does not create an absolute prohibition against racial preferences, "[i]t does not, however, preclude a state from providing greater protection" against discrimination. Unlike the federal equal protection clause as interpreted by the U.S. Supreme Court, Brown explained, the California Constitution absolutely "prohibits discrimination and preferential treatment. Its literal language admits no 'compelling state interest' exception; we find nothing to suggest the voters intended to include one sub silentio."[34]

In *San Remo Hotel L.P. v. City and County of San Francisco*, the court validated the city's requirement that a hotel seeking to move from short-term to long-term residential use replace the units that were available to daily tenants. Dissenting, Justice Brown remarked that "private property, already an endangered species in California, is now entirely extinct in San Francisco." Brown noted that the purpose of the law was to provide affordable housing for low-income residents. "The most egalitarian way to achieve this goal would be to distribute the cost of subsidies as broadly as possible," she observed, "but the forces attacking private property in California—though claiming the moral high ground—have proved themselves anything but egalitarian in their approach."[35] Though the requirement clearly was unconstitutional under the Fifth Amendment, it also violated the California Constitution, Brown argued. "This is *not* a tough case. . . . San Francisco has expropriated the property and resources of a few hundred hotel operators in order to ameliorate—off budget and out of sight of the taxpayer—its housing shortage."[36] Brown lamented: "Theft is still theft even when the government approves of the thievery. Turning a democracy into a kleptocracy does not enhance the stature of the thieves; it only diminishes the legitimacy of the government."[37]

Justice Brown also dissented from a decision upholding a statute that required employers to cover contraceptives in their health insurance policies, even if they objected on religious grounds. Brown found that the mandate violated not only the First Amendment but also the religion provisions of the California Constitution. The state constitution has independent force, Brown argued, which "is true even when the language is identical to the federal Constitution, but is particularly true when the language differs."[38] Whatever the outcome under the U.S. Constitution, Brown believed that the court should have applied the more sweeping state constitutional language to prevent the coercion.[39]

Regrettably Justices Sanders and Brown are found too often on the dissenting side of cases. That is natural because they are legal pioneers, seeking to rediscover and vigorously apply the principles underlying the constitutions that set forth the first principles of our republican government. Their bold and principled decisions, as well as the underlying constitutional provisions themselves, underscore the realm of the possible for those who seek greater judicial protection for liberty. But a metamorphosis in state constitutional law can occur only if the freedom movement files cases and makes arguments to vindicate the great untapped promise of state constitutions.

11. An Activist Judiciary, for All the Right Reasons

If you've read all the preceding 10 chapters and remain unconvinced that we need, and that our Constitution provides for, a judiciary that acts aggressively to curb tyranny and protect individual rights, I can only recommend one final recourse: go see a movie.

Not just any movie, but a delightful Australian flick called *The Castle*, which you can find at some good video rental stores. It's a sweet film that evokes both tears and laughter. And it's so moving that on several occasions the Institute for Justice has rented movie theaters to show the film in communities where the institute is waging legal battles against eminent domain abuse.

The movie is about a very ordinary family living in Australia. Their home is fairly ramshackle, with massive power lines in the backyard. They live adjacent to a runway of a large international airport, and the noise is deafening. But their home is their castle, where they have raised their children and their dogs and which contains the rich memories of a lifetime.

Everything is fine until a powerful consortium decides it needs land near the airport. So the authorities decide to use eminent domain—in Australia it's called "compulsory acquisition"—to obtain the land. The family and their neighbors are certain that can't happen—after all, it's their property. The company makes paltry settlement offers it condescendingly characterizes as generous, and the company's lawyers can't understand why the people don't want to move. The families pool their resources and hire a lawyer, who fails miserably in the trial court. Only then do the families realize how few rights they have and how easily those rights can be taken away by voracious governments acting on behalf of favored interests. As one of the characters remarks, the government is not taking their house, it's taking their home.

I won't give away the movie's ending, except to say that the hero is a constitutional lawyer, which probably is one of the reasons I love it so much. And of course the movie is not fiction at all—the scenario plays out every day, not just in Australia but in the United States and certainly in other self-styled liberal democracies around the world.

What is more fiction than reality is that it has a happy ending. Too often real people when faced with government oppression have no idea how to fight back. They lack the time, the resources, or the experience to organize the community toward political action. They don't have the money to hire lawyers. If they approach city hall, their legislature, or God forbid, Congress, they come away empty-handed. Too often, that's the result in court as well. This book highlights the courageous and heroic actions of individuals who have stood up for their rights, often successfully. But far more typically, the abuse of individual rights is like the proverbial tree falling in the forest: it doesn't make a sound because the only people who hear it are the victims themselves, who endure it in silent anguish.

I'll never forget when I went to visit the shoeshine entrepreneur Ego Brown to propose filing a constitutional challenge on his behalf. He knew that the law that had put him out of business was unfair. But it never occurred to him that his constitutional rights had been violated or that he might have legal recourse. To be sure, some people believe that every injustice visited upon them is a violation of their constitutional rights. But most people are like Ego Brown, assuming that if their elected officials do something, they must have the power to do it. The power, yes, but in a free society, not necessarily the legitimate authority. And in a constitutional democracy, the role of determining the lines of demarcation between power and authority lies ultimately with the courts.

In the first instance, of course, the responsibility to police constitutional boundaries lies with elected officials themselves. After all, they take an oath to uphold the Constitution. I suspect that, too often, the feelings that accompany the uttering of those words are not humility but a power rush; if not then, it comes later. Long lost to a bygone era are great debates among elected officials about the constitutional limits of their powers. Just as ordinary people rarely suspect that government actions might violate their constitutional rights, seldom do government officials believe their exercise of power might transgress constitutional boundaries. If the exercise of government power serves the public good as the officials see it, then it must be constitutional. Certainly the judicial presumption in favor of the constitutionality of government actions fuels such hubris.

But that is the appropriate starting point: a friendly reminder to government officials, both elected and appointed, that limits to their powers exist—and consequences for abusing them. An automatic, serious, self-initiated process of careful reflection among government officials should be triggered every time they exercise power that affects the lives of individuals—and not a mere rubber-stamping of proposed action by government lawyers, who frequently forget that their first responsibility is not to the officials who hired them but to the citizens themselves. But in practice it is not that way; hence frequent reminders are necessary.

Unfortunately, the reminders often need to take the form of litigation. One of the ways in which the system is skewed in favor of government and against individuals is that officials usually are immune from personal consequences for actions taken in their governmental capacities. Fortunately, one substitute for personal culpability is the prospect for recovering attorneys' fees, which can have a chastening effect on government officials as well. A government official who not only has had an action invalidated by a court but has exposed the public fisc to attorneys' fees is one who may not be so inclined to excess next time (or, better yet, is introduced to the joys of retirement by the electorate).

But that type of outcome requires a judiciary that doesn't sit on its hands. Again, through such doctrines as standing and presumption of constitutionality, the odds are against individuals who challenge government action. The overwhelming majority of the civil cases faced by judges are routine disputes far removed from constitutional implications. Yet in the rare but important cases brought before them that do raise serious constitutional issues, judges should see themselves as what they are intended to be: fearless guardians of individual liberty. They are our system's insurance policy against its own natural abuses.

When a judge takes an oath to uphold the Constitution, it implies two mutually reinforcing obligations: to *enforce* the *Constitution*. The first obligation is an active one; the second, a constraining one.

The Constitution gives the judiciary the power and duty to police the actions of the other branches of government to ensure their conformity to the Constitution. Many judges laudably are humble people, aware of their vast power and deferential to democratic processes. It is essential to the legitimacy of the judiciary and to the rule of law that judges exercise judicial powers and not executive and legislative ones. But the ultimate deference must be to the Constitution, which is superior to the power of all branches of government. When an action of government is challenged as exceeding the scope of permissible power or invading individual liberty, the judge should not shrink from the necessary role of examining it in the context of constitutional commands. Excessive deference to government power equals judicial abdication of constitutional duties and results in tyranny meant not to be tolerated in our constitutional system. Although our system does not contemplate judges who are philosopher-kings, nor can it long survive judges who are rubber stamps for the executive and legislative branches.

By the Constitution is meant not some abstract, amorphous, or shifting philosophical ideal, but the words, plain meaning, and intent of the Framers, as applied to contemporary circumstances. That requires giving meaning to every word of the Constitution and attempting in good faith to discern that meaning. It also means hewing to what appears in the Constitution rather than what does not. Our constitutional jurisprudence holds that a right to welfare appears in the Constitution, when it does not; and that limiting the power of eminent domain to property acquired for public use does not appear in the Constitution, when it does. Sometimes the answers are not easy or obvious. That is where the Framers' design comes in, requiring judges to indulge not a presumption in favor of government power to which individual rights are the exception, a concept alien to the Framers, but the presumption in favor of liberty that is reflected in the words of the Constitution.

Some would argue that we are so far away from the original design that it is dangerous to entrust judges with power they can so recklessly exercise. Others argue that returning to original meaning would require sweeping nullification of laws on the books. Those objections are as nothing compared to the human consequences of the judiciary's failure to vindicate its vital role as a check on excessive government power and a safeguard for individual liberty, as several of the preceding chapters illustrate. By emasculating judicial power, as some conservatives urge, we remove the ultimate protection against abuse of rights by the other branches of government. The reluctance to reconsider past decisions or to strike down excessive government power, championed by many liberals, amounts to constitutional amendment without popular ratification and gives rise to rampant abuses of individual rights.

Neither side need worry that its most terrifying visions will come to pass. The change in direction suggested here—a midcourse correction of sorts—is by nature evolutionary, not revolutionary. Courts consider cases one at a time and rarely announce sweeping, wholesale changes. Even so significant a change as overturning the *Slaughter-House Cases* and restoring the lost constitutional language of the privileges or immunities clause would substitute a means/ends balancing for complete judicial abdication—a substantial difference from the status quo, to be sure, but far from overturning the edifice of the modern welfare state. It seems a far greater exercise of judicial arrogance to ignore constitutional text that clearly was intended to mean something significant than to attempt to discern and apply its meaning in good faith, even if that latter endeavor thrusts the judiciary into a more activist role. The Framers of both the original Constitution and the Fourteenth Amendment emphatically did not intend the courts to be handmaidens to an ever-enlarging government and to ever-growing encroachments into the realm of individual autonomy.

Moreover, the judiciary itself is checked by democratic forces; if it strays too far from the popular consensus or moves too far, too fast, the people will rein it in. The difference in public sentiment toward the Warren Court on the one hand and the Rehnquist Court on the other suggests that the principles embraced by our Constitution seem to enjoy popular support even today. Judicial lawlessness that transcends the boundaries of legitimate judicial power and creates new rights out of thin air, exemplified by the Warren Court, seems to excite people in a negative way. By contrast, judicial activism that restores the Constitution to its original meaning, a direction that the Rehnquist Court generally followed, seems to disturb most people not at all. Indeed, although the Rehnquist Court provoked hysteria among the left, only in two instances did it stir significant public backlash: when it appeared poised to overturn a widely supported liberty, a precipice from which the Court retreated when it reaffirmed *Roe v. Wade*, and when it failed to apply its newfound protection for private property rights to curb eminent domain abuse.

Even the Court's controversial decision in *Bush v. Gore* seemed to evoke feelings of relief rather than outrage among an exhausted electorate. Such public reaction indicates that, generally speaking, the American people like courts that do what they are supposed to do: to enforce the Constitution and protect individual rights.

The path of the Roberts Court is not yet clear. The Court will have ample opportunity to resume and even accelerate the course of its predecessor in restoring to the judiciary its intended role as a guardian of freedom. For even as the Rehnquist Court lost its momentum in its waning days, the intellectual energy among pro-freedom academics and policy organizations continues to grow, and it will provide the Court with abundant opportunities to restore constitutional limits on government power and lost individual liberties. The Court's recent decision striking down Vermont's campaign contribution limits certainly is a hopeful sign that, at least in some areas, it will stake out new ground in the protection of individual freedoms. The Court remains closely divided, but every justice has proven capable of supplying pro-freedom votes in any given case. And patrolling the Court's libertarian center is Justice Anthony Kennedy, who has shown himself in many cases to be extremely mindful of the need for an activist judiciary to protect individual rights.

Nonetheless, the Court today operates at a time of perceived emergency and the concomitant demands for emergency government powers that always seem to accompany it. The present crisis poses greater danger to liberty than past ones, for our war against terrorism is undeclared and potentially infinite, and the means employed to ferret out the enemy bode dangerous consequences for individual liberty. I remember attending a Federalist Society national lawyers' convention a few years ago and hearing a Justice Department lawyer assure the audience that the Bush administration would respect individual liberty in its enforcement of anti-terrorism laws and that the president would let us know when the emergency was over. Although the words were intended to be comforting, history counsels abundantly that we must place our trust not in the person who inhabits the White House at any particular time but with the Constitution. Hence even as demands for judicial deference are loudest, the role of the courts in protecting individual liberty necessarily is at its apex in time of crisis.

A good start toward restoring the judiciary to its intended course is for both the right and the left to get over their antipathy toward principled judicial activism. If groups such as the American Civil Liberties Union want the courts zealously to protect freedom of speech and the rights of criminal defendants, they need to accept that the courts also must protect private property rights and freedom of contract. Likewise, if conservatives want courts to protect economic liberties, they must also accept that the courts must protect the rights of people to engage in nonharmful, consensual activities in their own homes and of political dissenters to burn the American flag. In short, if we want protections for the liberties we most care about, we must tolerate protections for the liberties other people care about. And where mechanisms of democratic self-restraint fail, we must accept the role of the courts in policing vigorously the constitutional limits on government power. An ad hoc jurisprudence that depends on whose rights are being gored—or, even worse, a judiciary that retreats altogether from policing the constitutional boundaries of the other branches of government—will destroy the rule of law on which both our republic's legitimacy and our liberties depend.

Are courts up to the task? Much depends on the men and women who are appointed, which in turn depends upon the officials who appoint and confirm them, and the opinions of the American people generally. The inability of groups such as People for the American Way to galvanize opposition to the nomination of Justice Samuel Alito is a useful barometer that indicates the American people generally are satisfied with the direction of the U.S. Supreme Court—even if it occasionally makes decisions with which the majority of Americans disagree. My own view is that when such decisions are firmly grounded in the Constitution, the Court's standing will remain strong; when they are not, such decisions bring the entire judicial enterprise into disrepute. The dividing line, then, is not between judicial activism and judicial restraint; it is between legitimate and vigorous judicial action and illegitimate judicial imperialism—hence the very different public sentiment toward the activism of the Warren Court and the activism of the Rehnquist Court.

The resolution of the questions posed in this book is of great consequence to the likes of Juanita Swedenburg, Ego Brown, and Susette Kelo—Americans who want nothing more from their government than to be left alone. When their government violates their rights, they must have recourse. Creating the power of judicial review, as the Framers of our Constitution saw fit to do, creates dangers. But that danger is not as great as its opposite: legislative and executive powers unchecked by judicial review. Yet that is the logical consequence of the most extreme views promoted on both the left and the right. The current system is messy and often frustrating. But to paraphrase Winston Churchill, it is the worst possible system—except for all the rest.

If I accomplish anything in this book, I hope it will be to help remove judicial activism from the realm of the epithet. We need a vigorous judiciary to remain free. The best tether to ensure that the judiciary stays focused on its proper role is the Constitution itself.

Notes

Chapter 1

1. William O. Douglas, *The Court Years 1939–1975: The Autobiography of William O. Douglas* (New York: Random House, 1980), p. 8.

2. For a superb overview of the perverse incentives and byproducts of the American legal system, see Robert A. Levy, *Shakedown: How Corporations, Government, and Trial Lawyers Abuse the Judicial Process* (Washington: Cato Institute, 2004).

3. Robert D. Atkinson, *The Revenge of the Disintermediated: How the Middleman Is Fighting E-Commerce and Hurting Consumers* (Washington: Progressive Policy Institute, 2001), www.ppionline.org/documents/disintermediated.pdf.

4. *Possible Barriers to E-Commerce: Wine*, A Report from the Staff of the Federal Trade Commission, July 2003, www.ftc.gov/os/2003/07/winereport2.pdf.

5. See, e.g., *Hunt v. Washington State Apple Advertising Comm'n*, 432 U.S. 333 (1977).

6. For an excellent and persuasive argument for the latter proposition, see Randy E. Barnett, *Restoring the Lost Constitution: The Presumption of Liberty* (Princeton, NJ: Princeton University Press, 2004).

7. *Bridenbaugh v. Freeman-Wilson*, 227 F.3d 848, 849 (7th Cir. 2000), cert. denied, 532 U.S. 1002 (2001).

8. *Bacchus Imports Ltd. v. Dias*, 468 U.S. 263, 276 (1984).

9. *Swedenburg v. Kelly*, 232 F. Supp. 2d 135, 145 (S.D.N.Y. 2002).

10. *Swedenburg*, 232 F. Supp. 2d at 148.

11. *Swedenburg*, 232 F. Supp. 2d at 150.

12. *Swedenburg v. Kelly*, 358 F.3d 223, 231 (2d Cir. 2004).

13. *Swedenburg*, 358 F.3d at 237.

14. See, e.g., *Camps Newfound/Owatonna, Inc. v. Town of Harrison*, 520 U.S. 564, 609–39 (1997) (Thomas, J., dissenting).

15. *Granholm v. Heald*, 125 S. Ct. 1885, 1891–92 (2005).

16. *Granholm*, 125 S. Ct. at 1896.

17. *Granholm*, 125 S. Ct. at 1897.

18. *Granholm*, 125 S. Ct. at 1904.

19. Joseph Kahn, "When Chinese Sue the State, Cases Are Often Smothered," *New York Times*, December 28, 2005, p. A1.

20. See, e.g., Robert H. Bork, ed., *A Country I Do Not Recognize: The Legal Assault on American Values* (Stanford, CA: Hoover Institution Press, 2005).

21. Quoted in Adam Liptak, "Justices' Public Comments Tending Toward Political," *Arizona Republic*, March 19, 2006, p. A4.

Chapter 2

1. Jeffrey Rosen, "It's the Law, Not the Judge," *Washington Post*, March 27, 2005, p. B1.

2. Quoted in Dave Denison, "Judging the Judges," *Boston Globe*, March 7, 2004, p. H1.

3. Quoted in Denison, "Judging the Judges."

4. Jonathan Rauch, "You Say You Want a Revolution," July 29, 2005, http://www.jonathanrauch.com/jrauch_articles/2005/07/you_say_you_wan.html.

5. Quoted in Wes Allison, "Courts May Feel Schiavo Impact," *St. Petersburg Times*, April 4, 2005.

6. Quoted in Jeffrey Rosen, "Out of Order," *The New Republic*, May 30, 2005, p. 12.

7. Quoted in Tatsha Robertson, "Gays, Lesbians Praise Decision—Others Compare It to Roe v. Wade," *Boston Globe*, June 27, 2003.

8. *Lawrence v. Texas*, 539 U.S. 558, 602 (2003) (Scalia, J., dissenting).

9. Quoted in Denison, "Judging the Judges."

10. Quoted in Jerry Seper, "Ashcroft Rips Federal Judges on National Security," *Washington Times*, November 13, 2004, p. A2.

11. Quoted in James Kuenhenn, "GOP Chiefs Reveal Division Concerning Role of Judiciary," *Pittsburgh Post-Gazette*, April 6, 2005, p. A-16.

12. Quoted in Carl Hulse and David D. Kirkpatrick, "DeLay Says Federal Judiciary Has 'Run Amok,' Adding Congress Is Partly to Blame," *New York Times*, April 8, 2005, p. 21.

13. A useful compendium of efforts past and present to bludgeon judges into political submission can be found in Maro Robbins, "Passing Judgment on Activist Judges," *San Antonio Express-News*, April 24, 2005, p. 1A.

14. Carolyn Lochhead, "House OK's Limit on Federal Courts," *San Francisco Chronicle*, July 23, 2004, p. A6.

15. Quoted in Jeffrey Rosen, "Obstruction of Judges," *New York Times*, August 11, 2002, p. 38.

16. Quoted in Tim Poor, "Ashcroft Denounces 'Judicial Despotism' by Federal Courts," *St. Louis Post-Dispatch*, March 6, 1997, p. 5A.

17. Mark R. Levin, *Men in Black: How the Supreme Court Is Destroying America* (Washington: Regnery Publishing, Inc., 2005), pp. 11–12.

18. Ibid., p. 12.

19. Ibid., p. 23.

20. Ibid., p. 26.

21. Ibid., p. 168.

22. Ibid., pp. 201–2.

23. Ibid., p. 131.

24. Charles Lane, "Evangelical Republicans Trust States on Social Issues," *Washington Post*, June 16, 2005.

25. John Yoo, "Bush Emerges as Federalism's Foe," *Newark (NJ) Star-Ledger*, June 23, 2005, p. 21. For a more comprehensive critique of the Bush administration's constitutional record, see Gene Healy and Timothy Lynch, "Power Surge: The Constitutional Record of George W. Bush," Cato Institute White Paper, May 1, 2006.

26. Ibid. For a more comprehensive critique of the Bush administration's constitutional record, see Gene Healy and Timothy Lynch, *Power Surge: The Constitutional Record of George W. Bush* (Washington: Cato Institute, 2006).

27. *New York Times Magazine*, April 17, 2005, cover.

28. Indeed, even Sunstein bought into the overheated rhetoric with the choice of title for his recent book. See Cass R. Sunstein, *Radicals in Robes: Why Extreme Right-Wing Courts Are Wrong for America* (New York: Basic Books, 2005).

29. Cass Sunstein and Randy Barnett debate, "Constitution in Exile," *Legal Affairs*, May 2–6, 2005, www.legalaffairs.org/webexclusive/debateclub_cie0505.msp.

30. Paul Gewirtz and Chad Golder, "So Who Are the Activists?" *New York Times*, July 6, 2005, p. A23.

31. *Chevron U.S.A., Inc. v. Natural Resources Defense Council, Inc.*, 467 U.S. 837 (1984).

32. *Chevron*, 467 U.S. 837, 844 (1984).

33. *Chevron*, 467 U.S. at 865–66.

34. *Chevron*, 467 U.S. at 844.

35. Stephen Breyer, *Active Liberty: Interpreting Our Democratic Constitution* (New York: Alfred A. Knopf, 2005), p. 6.

36. Ibid., p. 16.

37. Ibid., pp. 5–6.

38. Ibid., p. 37.

39. Ibid., p. 49.

40. *Zelman v. Simmons-Harris*, 536 U.S. 639 (2002).

41. Breyer, *Active Liberty*, pp. 120–21.

Chapter 3

1. For an excellent distillation of the proper role of the judiciary under our Constitution, see Roger Pilon, "Restoring Constitutional Government," *Cato Supreme Court Review* 1 (2002): vii.

2. See Philip Hamburger, "Law and Judicial Duty," *George Washington Law Review* 72, no. 1/2 (2003): 1.

3. See William R. Casto, "James Iredell and the American Origins of Judicial Review," *Connecticut Law Review* 27 (1995): 329.

4. Quoted in Randy E. Barnett, "James Madison's Ninth Amendment," in *The Rights Retained by the People*, ed. Randy E. Barnett (Fairfax, VA: George Mason University Press, 1989), p. 21.

5. Quoted in *The Great Debate: Interpreting Our Written Constitution* (Washington: The Federalist Society, 1986), p. 16.

6. James Madison, "The Federalist No. 10." In Alexander Hamilton, John Jay, and James Madison, *The Federalist*, Modern College Library Edition (New York: Random House) p. 54.

7. "The Federalist No. 10," p. 55.

8. "The Federalist No. 10," p. 55.

9. "The Federalist No. 10," p. 56.

10. "The Federalist No. 10," pp. 56–57.

11. "The Federalist No. 10," p. 58.

12. See Clint Bolick, *Leviathan: The Growth of Local Government and the Erosion of Liberty* (Stanford, CA: Hoover Institution Press, 2004); and *Grassroots Tyranny: The Limits of Federalism* (Washington: Cato Institute, 1993).

13. Quoted in William J. Brennan Jr., "The Bill of Rights and the States: The Revival of State Constitutions as Guardians of Individual Rights," *New York University Law Review* 61 (1986): 535, 536–37.

14. "The Federalist No. 10," pp. 60–61.

15. "The Federalist No. 10," pp. 57–58.

16. Alexander Hamilton, "The Federalist No. 78," p. 504. Emphasis in original.

17. Quoted in Stephen Macedo, *The New Right and the Constitution* (Washington: Cato Institute, 1986), p. 26. Emphasis in original.

18. "The Federalist No. 78," p. 508.

19. "The Federalist No. 78," p. 506.

20. "The Federalist No. 78," p. 508.

21. "The Federalist No. 78," p. 505.

22. "The Federalist No. 78," pp. 505–6.

23. Quoted in Eyler Robert Coates Sr., ed., *Thomas Jefferson on Politics & Government*, http://etext.virginia.edu/jefferson/quotations/jeff0950.htm.

24. Randy E. Barnett, ed., *The Rights Retained by the People* (Fairfax, VA: George Mason University Press, 1989), p. 34.

25. James Madison, "Speech to the House," in *The Rights Retained by the People*, ed. Randy E. Barnett, p. 61.

26. Barnett, *The Rights Retained*, p. 41.

27. Madison, "Speech to the House," in Barnett, *The Rights Retained*, p. 61.

28. *Marbury v. Madison*, 5 U.S. 137, 177 (1803).

29. *Marbury v. Madison*, 5 U.S. at 174.

30. *Marbury v. Madison*, 5 U.S. at 178.

31. *Barron v. Mayor and City Council of Baltimore*, 32 U.S. 243, 250 (1833).

32. Michael Kent Curtis, *No State Shall Abridge* (Durham, NC: Duke University Press, 1986), p. 41.

33. For a more in-depth examination of the respective powers of the national and state governments in the constitutional system of federalism, see Bolick, *Grassroots Tyranny*, pp. 13–92.

34. *Congressional Globe*, 39th Cong., 1st Sess., 1866, H. p. 1832.

35. Quoted in Christopher L. Eisgruber, "Marbury, Marshall, and the Politics of Constitutional Judgment," *Virginia Law Review* 89 (2003): 1203, 1227.

36. Jeffrey Rosen, *The Most Democratic Branch: How the Courts Serve America* (New York: Oxford University Press, 2006).

37. See Michael B. Rappaport, "Reconciling Textualism and Federalism: The Proper Textual Basis of the Supreme Court's Tenth and Eleventh Amendment Decisions," *Northwestern University Law Review* 93 (1999): 819, 822–23.

38. Cass Sunstein and Randy Barnett debate, "Constitution in Exile," *Legal Affairs*, May 2–6, 2005, www.legalaffairs.org/webexclusive/debateclub_cie0505.msp.

Chapter 4

1. Nevertheless, my friends Bob Levy and Chip Mellor have endeavored to do exactly that. See Robert A. Levy and William H. Mellor, *The Dirty Dozen: A Non-Lawyer's Guide to the Worst Supreme Court Cases of the Modern Era* (forthcoming).

2. *The Slaughter-House Cases*, 83 U.S. 36 (1873).

3. *Plessy v. Ferguson*, 163 U.S. 537, 550–51 (1896).

4. *Plessy*, 163 U.S. at 554 (Harlan, J., dissenting).

5. *Plessy*, 163 U.S. at 559 (Harlan, J., dissenting).

6. An excellent synopsis of this constitutional metamorphosis is provided by Richard A. Epstein, *How Progressives Rewrote the Constitution* (Washington: Cato Institute, 2006).

7. *Home Building & Loan Ass'n v. Blaisdell*, 290 U.S. 398, 425 (1934).

8. *Blaisdell*, 290 U.S. at 428.

9. *Blaisdell*, 290 U.S. at 428.

10. *Blaisdell*, 290 U.S. at 440.

11. *Blaisdell*, 290 U.S. at 443–44.

12. *Blaisdell*, 290 U.S. at 448–49 (Sutherland, J., dissenting).

13. Again, those rights were intended to be protected under the privileges or immunities clause (see chapter 7).

14. *U.S. v. Carolene Products*, 304 U.S. 144, 152 (1938).

15. *Carolene Products*, 304 U.S. at 153 n.4.

16. Randy E. Barnett, *Restoring the Lost Constitution: The Presumption of Liberty* (Princeton, NJ: Princeton University Press, 2004), pp. 278–318.

17. *Schechter Poultry Corp. v. United States*, 295 U.S. 495, 528 (1935).

18. *Schechter Poultry*, 295 U.S. at 529.

19. *Schechter Poultry*, 295 U.S. at 546.

20. *Wickard v. Filburn*, 317 U.S. 111, 128 (1942).

21. *Korematsu v. United States*, 323 U.S. 214, 219–20 (1944).

22. *Korematsu*, 323 U.S. at 225.

23. *Korematsu*, 323 U.S. at 219.

24. *Korematsu*, 323 U.S. at 245–46 (Jackson, J., dissenting).

25. See Clint Bolick, *The Affirmative Action Fraud: Can We Restore the American Civil Rights Vision?* (Washington: Cato Institute, 1996), pp. 51–68.

26. *Swann v. Charlotte-Mecklenburg Board of Education*, 402 U.S. 1, 16 (1971). For a fuller discussion of the excesses of desegregation jurisprudence, see Bolick, *The Affirmative Action Fraud*, pp. 69–81.

27. State courts, too, have assumed operational authority of schools over violations of state constitutional provisions. See, e.g., *Serrano v. Priest*, 487 P.2d 1241 (Cal. 1971); *Robinson v. Cahill*, 202 A.2d 273 (NJ 1973). The New Jersey courts have been essentially running many schools in that state for nearly four decades.

28. See, e.g., *Ruiz v. Estelle*, 503 F. Supp. 1265 (S.D. Tex. 1980).

29. *Miranda v. Arizona*, 384 U.S. 436 (1966).

30. *Goldberg v. Kelly*, 397 U.S. 254, 263 n.8 (1970).

31. *Goldberg*, 397 U.S. at 273 (Black, J., dissenting).

32. *Goldberg*, 397 U.S. at 274 (Black, J., dissenting).

33. *Goldberg*, 397 U.S. at 276 (Black, J., dissenting).

34. For an examination of the practice and consequences of courts' assuming executive and legislative powers, see Ross Sandler and David Schoenbrod, *Democracy by Decree: What Happens When Courts Run Government* (New Haven, CT: Yale University Press, 2003).

35. *Pierce v. Society of Sisters of the Holy Names of Jesus and Mary*, 268 U.S. 510, 534–35 (1925).

36. Interestingly, the Court in *Carolene Products* singled out *Pierce* as a case that encompassed the realm of liberties appropriately protected by the Court. The Court, however, wrongly explained the case as one in which particular religions were targeted, which was not true—the Court forbade all private schools, both secular and religious. Indeed, in addition to the Society of Sisters, the other named plaintiff was Hill Military Academy, whose interests were not likely religious in nature.

37. *West Virginia State Board of Education v. Barnette*, 319 U.S. 624, 631 (1943)

38. *Barnette*, 319 U.S. at 640.

39. *Barnette*, 319 U.S. at 638.

40. *Barnette*, 319 U.S. at 639–40.

41. *Barnette*, 319 U.S. at 639–40.
42. *Barnette*, 319 U.S. at 642.
43. *Brown v. Board of Education*, 347 U.S. 483 (1954).
44. *Roe v. Wade*, 410 U.S. 113 (1973).
45. *Brown*, 347 U.S. 483, 493 (1954).
46. *Griswold v. Connecticut*, 381 U.S. 479, 484 (1965).
47. *Griswold*, 381 U.S. at 486.
48. *Griswold*, 381 U.S. at 486–87 (Goldberg, J., concurring).
49. *Griswold*, 381 U.S. at 491 (Goldberg, J., concurring).
50. *Stanley v. Georgia*, 394 U.S. 557, 565 (1969).
51. *Wisconsin v. Yoder*, 406 U.S. 205, 214 (1972).
52. The Warren Court's liberal majority survived for several years the replacement of Chief Justice Warren.
53. *Yoder*, 406 U.S. at 218.
54. *Yoder*, 406 U.S. at 232.
55. *Va. State Bd. of Pharmacy v. Va. Citizens Consumers Council, Inc.*, 425 U.S. 748, 770 (1976).

Chapter 5

1. The history and evolution of the conservative public interest law movement are chronicled in Lee Edwards, ed., *Bringing Justice to the People: The Story of the Freedom-Based Public Interest Law Movement* (Washington: Heritage Books, 2004), and in a fascinating law review article, Ann Southworth, "Conservative Lawyers and the Contest Over the Meaning of 'Public Interest Law,'" *UCLA Law Review* 52 (2005): 1223.

2. Recently, liberals have launched a competing organization, the American Constitution Society, which has further enriched intellectual vitality in law schools and the legal profession.

3. I profile several cases litigated by these groups, particularly Institute for Justice, in chapters 7, 8, and 9.

4. Described in Jonathan Rauch, "You Say You Want a Revolution," *National Journal*, July 29, 2005, http://nationaljournal.com/about/njweekly/stories/2005/0729nj1.htm.

5. Rauch, "You Say You Want a Revolution."

6. For a thematic treatment of Justice Scalia's record on the Court, see Ralph A. Rossum, *Antonin Scalia's Jurisprudence: Text and Tradition* (Lawrence, KS: University Press of Kansas, 2006). Professor Rossum characterizes Scalia as a textualist and traditionalist; that is, he is guided by the constitutional text and the tradition that existed at the time of adoption.

7. Institute for Justice, *State of the Supreme Court 2000: The Justices' Record on Individual Liberties* (Washington: Institute for Justice, 2000). The report can be found on the institute's website, www.ij.org.

8. Of course, Justice O'Connor subsequently strayed from her adherence to racial neutrality in *Grutter v. Bollinger*, the 2003 University of Michigan law school racial preference case.

9. Jeffrey Rosen, "Stare Decisis," *The New Republic*, September 19, 2005, p. 12.

10. Edward Lazarus, "Kennedy Center," *The New Republic*, November 14, 2005, p. 17.

11. Jonathan Rauch, "You Say You Want a Revolution."

12. *Bd. of Educ. of Oklahoma City Public Schools v. Dowell*, 498 U.S. 237, 247 (1991).

13. *Freeman v. Pitts*, 503 U.S. 467, 490 (1992).

14. *Missouri v. Jenkins*, 515 U.S. 70 (1995). See also Clint Bolick, *The Affirmative Action Fraud: Can We Restore the American Civil Rights Vision?* (Washington: Cato Institute, 1996), p. 75.

15. *Texas v. Johnson*, 491 U.S. 397, 406 (1989). Emphasis in original.

16. *Texas v. Johnson*, 491 U.S. at 414.

17. *McConnell v. Federal Election Commission*, 540 U.S. 93 (2003).

18. As this book was going to press, the Roberts Court decided *Randall v. Sorrell*, 126 S. Ct. 2479 (2006), striking down Vermont's draconian limits on campaign spending and contributions. As usual in this area of law, the decision was muddled, with individual justices heading off in multiple directions. Although a majority of justices declined to reconsider the Court's past jurisprudence, six of them (Chief Justice Roberts and Justices Kennedy, Scalia, Thomas, Breyer, and Alito) voted to strike down the restrictions, thereby restoring some protection to individual campaign contributions as a form of protected political expression. Justice Breyer's plurality opinion, while perhaps surprising to some, was previewed in his book, *Active Liberty: Interpreting Our Democratic Constitution* (New York: Alfred A. Knopf, 2005), which noted "the risk that reform legislation will defeat the participatory self-government objective itself," as when "laws set contribution limits so low that they elevate the . . . advantages of incumbency to the point of insulating incumbent officeholders from effective challenge." Id., p. 49. Although such a narrow protection and subjective analysis would do little to reinvigorate First Amendment protections in this area, the ruling as a whole is an encouraging sign that the Roberts Court may take up where the Rehnquist Court left off in expanding judicial protection of individual liberties.

19. *Boy Scouts of America v. Dale*, 530 U.S. 640 (2000).

20. *Bowers v. Hardwick*, 478 U.S. 186 (1986).

21. *Boy Scouts*, 530 U.S. at 655 (2000).

22. *Boy Scouts*, 530 U.S. at 649.

23. Justice O'Connor concurred in the result, expressing the view that the law should be struck down on equal protection grounds because it discriminated against homosexual as opposed to heterosexual sodomy.

24. *Bowers*, 478 U.S. at 190.

25. *Lawrence v. Texas*, 539 U.S. 558, 567 (2003). For an excellent analysis of the broader implications of this decision, which grounds the rights at issue in terms of liberty rather than privacy (as do the more recent abortion decisions), see Randy E. Barnett, "Justice Kennedy's Libertarian Revolution," *Cato Supreme Court Review* 2 (2003): 21.

26. *Lawrence*, 539 U.S. at 562.

27. *Lawrence*, 539 U.S. at 591 (Scalia, J., dissenting).

28. *Lawrence*, 539 U.S. at 603 (Scalia, J., dissenting).

29. *Romer v. Evans*, 517 U.S. 620, 623 (1996).

30. *Romer v. Evans*, 517 U.S. at 627.

31. *Romer v. Evans*, 517 U.S. at 636 and 652 (Scalia, J., dissenting).

32. *United States v. Virginia*, 518 U.S. 515, 533 (1996).

33. *U.S. v. Va.*, 518 U.S. at 542 (citation omitted).

34. *U.S. v. Va.*, 518 U.S. at 550. Emphasis in original.

35. *Wygant v. Jackson Bd. of Educ.*, 476 U.S. 267 (1986).

36. *Wygant* was the first case that I successfully brought to the U.S. Supreme Court, early in my career at Mountain States Legal Foundation. When the petition for review was under consideration, I was being recruited by the Reagan administration. I told Charles Cooper, then a deputy assistant attorney general, that if the Court granted review in *Wygant* and I couldn't argue it because I had switched jobs, I would kill myself. Cooper, usually sage in his legal prognostications, replied: "You can leave the razor blades in the closet, Clint. The Court will not grant review in *Wygant*." I ended up watching the argument from the visitor gallery. But I thought better of my vow and somehow have managed to live happily ever after.

37. *City of Richmond v. J.A. Croson Co.*, 488 U.S. 469, 520 (Scalia, J., concurring in the judgment).

38. *Adarand Constructors, Inc. v. Pena*, 515 U.S. 200 (1995).

39. *Adarand*, 515 U.S. at 239 (Scalia, J., concurring in part and concurring in the judgment).

40. *Gratz v. Bollinger*, 539 U.S. 244 (2003).

41. *Grutter v. Bollinger*, 539 U.S. 306, 343 (2003).

42. I have argued elsewhere, particularly in an earlier book, *The Affirmative Action Fraud*, against allowing governmental entities to use the easy out of racial preferences to cosmetically paper over severe inequalities in educational opportunities at the K–12 level. Such preferences impede or delay the adoption of systemic reforms, such as school choice, that can reduce the racial disparities that manifest themselves in university admissions and elsewhere. By upholding racial preferences, Justice O'Connor virtually guaranteed that such measures will still be in demand far into the future.

43. *Grutter*, 539 U.S. at 389 (Kennedy, J., dissenting).

44. *Grutter*, 539 U.S. at 370 and 378 (Thomas, J., concurring in part and dissenting in part).

45. *United States v. Lopez*, 514 U.S. 549, 552 (1995) (citation omitted).

46. *Lopez*, 514 U.S. at 559.

47. *Lopez*, 514 U.S. at 561.

48. *Lopez*, 514 U.S. at 564.

49. *Lopez*, 514 U.S. at 578 (Kennedy, J., concurring).

50. *Lopez*, 514 U.S. at 585 (Thomas, J., concurring).

51. *United States v. Morrison*, 529 U.S. 598, 617 (2000).

52. In a concurring opinion, Justice Scalia grounded the congressional authority to bootstrap intrastate economic activity to regulation of interstate commerce in its power under the Constitution to enact legislation that is "necessary and proper" to effectuate its authority. *Gonzales v. Raich*, 125 S. Ct. 2195, 2218–20 (2005) (Scalia, J., concurring in the judgment).

53. *Gonzales*, 125 S. Ct. at 2205 (citations omitted).

54. *Gonzales*, 125 S. Ct. at 2221 (O'Connor, J., dissenting).

Chapter 6

1. For a compilation of Justice Thomas's jurisprudence, see Henry Mark Holzer, *The Supreme Court Opinions of Clarence Thomas, 1991–2006* (Jefferson, NC: McFarland, 2007).

2. *McIntyre v. Ohio Elections Comm'n*, 514 U.S. 334, 378 (1995) (Scalia, J., dissenting).

3. *McIntyre*, 514 U.S. at 370 (Thomas, J., concurring in the judgment).

4. *McIntyre*, 514 U.S. at 370 (Thomas, J., concurring in the result).

5. *Van Orden v. Perry*, 545 U.S. 677, 125 S. Ct. 2854, 2865 (2005) (Thomas, J., concurring).

6. *Van Orden*, 125 S. Ct. at 2866 (Thomas, J., concurring).

7. *Van Orden*, 125 S. Ct. at 2867 (Thomas, J., concurring).

8. *Saenz v. Roe*, 526 U.S. 489, 521 (1999) (Thomas, J., dissenting).

9. *Saenz*, 526 U.S. at 527–28 (Thomas, J., dissenting).

10. *Troxel v. Granville*, 530 U.S. 57, 91 (2000) (Scalia, J., dissenting).

11. *Troxel*, 530 U.S. at 80 (Thomas, J., concurring in the judgment).

12. *United States v. Lopez*, 514 U.S. 549, 589 (1995) (Thomas, J., concurring).

13. *Lopez*, 514 U.S. at 589 (Thomas, J., concurring). Emphasis in original.

14. *Lopez*, 514 U.S. at 601–2 (Thomas, J., concurring).

15. *United States v. Morrison*, 529 U.S. 598, 627 (2000) (Thomas, J., concurring).

16. *Gonzales v. Raich*, 125 S. Ct. 2195, 2229 (2005) (Thomas, J., dissenting).

17. *Raich*, 125 S. Ct. at 2236 (Thomas, J., dissenting).

18. *Gonzales v. Oregon*, 126 S. Ct. 904, 939 (2006) (Thomas, J., dissenting).

19. *Gonzales*, 126 S. Ct. at 940 (Thomas, J., dissenting).

20. *Gonzales*, 126 S. Ct. at 941 (Thomas, J., dissenting).

Chapter 7

1. *Congressional Globe*, 39th Cong., 1st sess., 1866, H. pp. 1151–52. For a general discussion of the nature of economic liberty, the history of its constitutional protection and evisceration, and a strategy to restore it, see Clint Bolick, *Unfinished Business: A Civil Rights Strategy for America's Third Century* (San Francisco: Pacific Research Institute, 1990), pp. 47–91.

2. *Congressional Globe*, 43rd Cong., 1st Sess., 1874, S. p. 3454.

3. *Corfield v. Coryell*, 6 F. Cas. 546 (C.C.E.D. Pa. 1823).

4. *Congressional Globe*, 42nd Cong., 1st sess., 1871, H. p. app. 86.

5. For a fascinating overview of the *Slaughter-House Cases* and their aftermath, see Charles A. Lofgren, *The Plessy Case* (New York: Oxford University Press, 1987).

6. *Slaughter-House Cases*, 83 U.S. 36, 75–79 (1873).

7. *Slaughter-House*, 83 U.S. at 87 (Field, J., dissenting).

8. *Slaughter-House*, 83 U.S. at 110 (Field, J., dissenting).

9. *Slaughter-House*, 83 U.S. at 125–30 (Swayne, J., dissenting).

10. See generally Lofgren, *The Plessy Case*.

11. For an excellent argument to protect the Bill of Rights through the privileges or immunities clause rather than the due process clause, see Michael Kent Curtis, *No State Shall Abridge* (Durham, NC: Duke University Press, 1986).

12. See David E. Bernstein, *Only One Place of Redress: African Americans, Labor Regulations, & the Courts from Reconstruction to the New Deal* (Durham, NC: Duke University Press, 2001).

13. *Yick Wo v. Hopkins*, 118 U.S. 356, 370 (1886).

14. *Lochner v. New York*, 198 U.S. 45, 56 (1905).

15. *Lochner*, 198 U.S. at 75 (Holmes, J., dissenting).

16. *West Coast Hotel Co. v. Parrish*, 300 U.S. 379, 391–400 (1937).

17. *West Coast Hotel*, 300 U.S. at 406 (Sutherland, J., dissenting).

18. *City of New Orleans v. Dukes*, 427 U.S. 297, 303–4 (1976).

19. *FCC v. Beach Communications, Inc.*, 508 U.S. 307, 314–15 (1993) (citations omitted).

20. *Beach Communications*, 508 U.S. at 315–16.

21. Because the District of Columbia is not a state, it is not subject to the Fourteenth Amendment.

22. *Brown v. Barry*, 710 F. Supp. 352, 355 (D.D.C. 1989). Emphasis in original.

23. *Brown v. Barry*, 710 F. Supp. at 356.

24. *Santos v. City of Houston*, 852 F. Supp. 601, 608 (S.D. Tex. 1994).

25. *Santos*, 852 F. Supp. at 608.

26. *Cornwell v. Hamilton*, 80 F. Supp. 2d 1101, 1106 (S.D. Cal. 1999).

27. *Cornwell*, 80 F. Supp. 2d at 1106.

28. *Craigmiles v. Giles*, 312 F.3d 220, 228 (6th Cir. 2002).

29. *Craigmiles*, 312 F.3d at 229.

30. *Powers v. Harris*, 379 F.3d 1208, 1220 (10th Cir. 2004).

31. *Powers*, 379 F.3d at 1221–22.

32. *Slaughter-House Cases*, 83 U.S. at 111 (Field, J., dissenting).

33. Antonin Scalia, "Economic Affairs as Human Affairs," in *Economic Liberties and the Judiciary*, ed. James A. Dorn and Henry G. Manne (Fairfax, VA: George Mason University Press, 1987), p. 37.

34. The leading Colorado proponent of taxicab deregulation was a state legislator, Bill Owens, who went on to serve two terms as Colorado's governor.

35. Kudos to John Kramer, the legendary maestro of media for the Institute for Justice. Whenever the institute loses a case in court, Kramer usually manages to win it in the court of public opinion.

Chapter 8

1. Elizabeth Rosenthal, "Factories Wrest Land from China's Farmers," *New York Times*, March 23, 2003, p. A10.

2. For an excellent distillation of the origin of American private property rights and the evolution of constitutional jurisprudence in this area, see Steven J. Eagle, "The Birth of the Property Rights Movement," Cato Institute Policy Analysis no. 558, December 15, 2005.

3. Dana Berliner, *Public Power, Private Gain* (Washington: Institute for Justice, 2003). The report can be found at http://castlecoalition.org/publications/report/index.html.

4. *Berman v. Parker*, 348 U.S. 26, 33 (1954).

5. *Berman*, 348 U.S. at 33.

6. *Hawaii Housing Auth. v. Midkiff*, 467 U.S. 229, 241 (1984) (internal citation omitted).

7. *Midkiff*, 467 U.S. at 241–42.

8. *Midkiff*, 467 U.S. at 245.

9. *United States v. James Daniel Good Real Property*, 510 U.S. 43, 61 (1993).

10. *Kelo v. City of New London*, 125 S. Ct. 2655, 2661 (2005) (internal citation omitted).

11. *Kelo*, 125 S. Ct. at 2662.

12. *Kelo*, 125 S. Ct. at 2663.

13. *Kelo*, 125 S. Ct. at 2672 (O'Connor, J., dissenting).

14. *Kelo*, 125 S. Ct. at 2672 (O'Connor, J., dissenting).

15. *Kelo*, 125 S. Ct. at 2675 (O'Connor, J., dissenting).

16. *Kelo*, 125 S. Ct. at 2675 (O'Connor, J., dissenting). Emphasis in original.

17. *Kelo*, 125 S. Ct. at 2675 (O'Connor, J., dissenting).

18. *Kelo*, 125 S. Ct. at 2677 (O'Connor, J., dissenting).

19. *Kelo*, 125 S. Ct. at 2678 (Thomas, J., dissenting).

20. *Kelo*, 125 S. Ct. at 2678 (Thomas, J., dissenting).

21. *Kelo*, 125 S. Ct. at 2684–85 (Thomas, J., dissenting).

22. Jonathan H. Adler, "Property Rights & Wrongs," *National Review Online*, June 29, 2005.

23. See, e.g., John M. Broder, "States Curbing Right to Seize Private Homes," *New York Times*, February 21, 2006, p. A1. Once again, the Institute for Justice deserves commendation for its superb efforts in the court of public opinion.

24. See John Tierney, "Supreme Court Home Makeover," *New York Times*, March 14, 2006, p. A1.

25. *Georgia v. Randolph*, 126 S. Ct. 1515, 1524 (2006).

26. *Pennsylvania Coal Co. v. Mahon*, 260 U.S. 393, 415 (1922).

27. *Nollan v. California Coastal Comm'n*, 483 U.S. 825, 837 (1987).

28. *Nollan*, 483 U.S. at 841.

29. *Lucas v. South Carolina Coastal Council*, 505 U.S. 1003 (1992).

30. *Dolan v. City of Tigard*, 512 U.S. 374, 391 (1994).

31. *Palazzolo v. Rhode Island*, 533 U.S. 606 (2001).

32. *Tahoe-Sierra Preservation Council, Inc. v. Tahoe Regional Planning Agency*, 535 U.S. 302, 335 (2002).

33. *Tahoe*, 535 U.S. at 342.

34. *Tahoe*, 535 U.S. at 343 (Rehnquist, C.J., dissenting).

35. See Clint Bolick, *Leviathan: The Growth of Local Government and the Erosion of Liberty* (Stanford, CA: Hoover Institution Press, 2004), pp. 83–99. One particularly egregious example is *Bennis v. Michigan*, 516 U.S. 442 (1996), which upheld the forfeiture of a woman's car that was used without her knowledge by her husband to solicit a prostitute, on the grounds that the car itself was the offender and constituted a public nuisance. The police thereby became richer and Mrs. Bennis suffered a double indignity.

Chapter 9

1. For an excellent exposition of the origins and intent of the First Amendment religion clauses, see Philip Hamburger, *Separation of Church and State* (Cambridge, MA: Harvard University Press, 2002).

2. For a more comprehensive discussion of that legal journey, see Clint Bolick, *Voucher Wars: Waging the Legal Battle over School Choice* (Washington: Cato Institute, 2003).

3. The tuition programs still exist, but they are limited to public and nonsectarian private schools. In my view, the exclusion of religious schools violates the First Amendment and the equal protection guarantee of the Fourteenth Amendment.

4. For more information about the nature, types, and effects of school choice, see www.allianceforschoolchoice.org.

5. *Committee for Public Education v. Nyquist*, 413 U.S. 756, 782 n.38 (1973).

6. *Mueller* was the first case in which I authored an amicus (friend of the court) brief, arguing that the "primary effect" of the program was not to advance religion, but to expand educational opportunities. That remained the central theme of my arguments over the course of the next 20 years of litigation over school choice.

7. *Mueller v. Allen*, 463 U.S. 388, 400 (1983).

8. *Witters v. Washington Dep't of Services for the Blind*, 474 U.S. 481, 490–91 (1986) (Powell, J., concurring).

9. *Zobrest v. Catalina Foothills School Dist.*, 509 U.S. 1 (1993).

10. *Jackson v. Benson*, 578 N.W.2d 602 (Wis. 1998).

11. *Kotterman v. Killian*, 972 P.2d 606 (Ariz. 1999).

12. *Simmons-Harris v. Goff*, 711 N.E.2d 203 (Ohio 1999).

13. *Rosenberger v. Rector and Visitors of Univ. of Va.*, 515 U.S. 819, 839 (1995).

14. *Rosenberger*, 515 U.S. at 886 (Souter, J., dissenting).

15. *Agostini v. Felton*, 521 U.S. 203, 231 (1997).

16. *Mitchell v. Helms*, 530 U.S. 793 (2000).

17. *Zelman v. Simmons-Harris*, 536 U.S. 639, 652 (2002).

18. *Zelman*, 536 U.S. at 680 (Thomas, J., concurring).

19. *Zelman*, 536 U.S. at 680 (Thomas, J., concurring).

20. *Zelman*, 536 U.S. at 684 (Thomas, J., concurring).

21. *Zelman*, 536 U.S. at 686 (Stevens, J., dissenting).

22. *Zelman*, 536 U.S. at 716 (Souter, J., dissenting).

23. *Zelman*, 536 U.S. at 717 (Breyer, J., dissenting).

24. *Zelman*, 536 U.S. at 662 n.7.

25. *Jackson*, 578 N.W.2d 602; *Kotterman*, 972 P.2d 606.

26. See, e.g., Steven K. Green, "The Blaine Amendment Reconsidered," *American Journal of Legal History* 36 (1992): 38.

27. *Mitchell*, 530 U.S. at 828–29 (plurality).

28. *Locke v. Davey*, 540 U.S. 712, 715 (2004).

29. One of the few but most important powers of the chief justice is the ability to assign opinions if he is in the majority. Chief Justice Rehnquist exercised that power adroitly (as when he assigned the *Zelman* decision to himself, which I believe helped keep Justice O'Connor in the fold because the tone of the opinion was very moderate, in stark contrast to the tone of the dissenters). Sometimes a chief justice will switch sides in order to assign the decision to himself so he can write it narrowly. Given Rehnquist's obvious disdain for Blaine amendments, as exhibited by the plurality decision in *Mitchell*, I believe he did that here, to make sure that future challenges to discriminatory applications of Blaine amendments were not foreclosed.

30. *Owens v. Colorado Congress of Parents*, 92 P.3d 933 (Colo. 2004); *Bush v. Holmes*, 919 So.2d 392 (Fla. 2006).

Chapter 10

1. *Bailey v. Myers*, 76 P.3d 898, 903 (Ariz. Ct. App. 2003).

2. *Bailey*, 76 P.3d at 902.

3. *Bailey*, 76 P.3d at 904.

4. *Poletown Neighborhood Council v. City of Detroit*, 304 N.W.2d 455, 459 (Mich. 1981).

5. For more about this sad story, see Clint Bolick, *Grassroots Tyranny: The Limits of Federalism* (Washington: Cato Institute, 1993), pp. 111–13.

6. *County of Wayne v. Hathcock*, 684 N.W.2d 765, 778 (Mich. 2004) (hereafter *Wayne County*).

7. *Wayne County*, 684 N.W.2d at 779.

8. *Wayne County*, 684 N.W.2d at 781. Emphasis in original.

9. *Wayne County*, 684 N.W.2d at 786.

10. *Wayne County*, 684 N.W.2d at 785.

11. *Wayne County*, 684 N.W.2d at 784.

12. Richard B. Sanders, "Battles for the State Constitution: A Dissenter's View," *Gonzaga Law Review* 37 (2001/2002): 1, 3.

13. William J. Brennan Jr., "State Constitutions and the Protection of Individual Rights," *Harvard Law Review* 90 (1977): 489, 491. (Justice Brennan often employed libertarian rhetoric, and sometimes he meant it. But the appeal of his argument to libertarians is obvious.)

14. William J. Brennan Jr., "The Bill of Rights and the States: The Revival of the State Constitution as Guardians of Individual Rights," *New York University Law Review* 61 (1986): 535, 537 (hereafter *N.Y.U. L. Rev.*).

15. Brennan, "Bill of Rights," *N.Y.U. L. Rev.* 61: 548.

16. Brennan, "State Constitutions," *Harvard Law Review* 90: 502.

17. Brennan, "Bill of Rights," *N.Y.U. L. Rev.* 61: 551.

18. Brennan, "Bill of Rights," *N.Y.U. L. Rev.* 61: 550.

19. Some libertarians disagree that victims' rights protections serve the ends of freedom. I make a case that they do in *Transformation: The Promise and Politics of Empowerment* (Oakland, CA: Institute for Contemporary Studies, 1998), pp. 144–46.

20. A classic example is *Bush v. Holmes*, 919 So.2d 392 (Fla. 2006), in which the Florida Supreme Court construed its state constitution in a tortured manner to strike down the opportunity scholarship program for children in failing public schools.

21. *Malyon v. Pierce County*, 935 P.2d 1272, 1274 (Wash. 1997).

22. *Malyon*, 935 P.2d at 1281–82.

23. *Malyon*, 935 P.2d at 1284.

24. *Open Door Baptist Church v. Clark County*, 995 P.2d 33, 48–49 (Sanders, J., dissenting).

25. *Open Door*, 995 P.2d at 50 (Sanders, J., dissenting).

26. *Open Door*, 995 P.2d at 51 (Sanders, J., dissenting).

27. *Gerberding v. Munro*, 949 P.2d 1366, 1379 (Wash. 1998) (Sanders, J., dissenting).

28. *Gerberding*, 949 P.2d at 1386 (Sanders, J., dissenting).

29. *State of Washington v. Ladson*, 979 P.2d 833, 839 (Wash. 1999).

30. *City of Seattle v. Mighty Movers, Inc.*, 96 P.3d 979, 990 (Wash. 2004) (Sanders, J., dissenting).

31. *Mighty Movers*, 96 P.3d at 992 (Sanders, J., dissenting).

32. *Aguilar v. Avis Rent a Car System*, 980 P.2d 846, 894 (Cal. 1999) (Brown, J., dissenting).

33. *Aguilar*, 980 P.2d at 895 (Brown, J., dissenting). Emphasis in original.

34. *Hi-Voltage Wire Works, Inc. v. City of San Jose*, 12 P.3d 1068, 1087 (Cal. 2000). I congratulate Pacific Legal Foundation for its fine work in support of the plaintiffs in this case.

35. *San Remo Hotel L.P. v. City and County of San Francisco*, 41 P.3d 87, 120 (Cal. 2002) (Brown, J., dissenting).

36. *San Remo Hotel*, 41 P.3d at 125–26 (Brown, J., dissenting). Emphasis in original.

37. *San Remo Hotel*, 41 P.3d at 128 (Brown, J., dissenting).

38. *Catholic Charities of Sacramento, Inc. v. Superior Court of Sacramento County*, 85 P.3d 67, 107 (Cal. 2004) (Brown, J., dissenting).

39. Justice Brown has moved on to the U.S. Court of Appeals for the District of Columbia, often considered the nation's second-most prominent court. I hope in her new capacity that Judge Brown will continue to exhibit the healthy skepticism toward abuses of government power that characterized her tenure on the California Supreme Court—a skepticism that is embodied in all American constitutions, both federal and state.

Index

Page references followed by n denote footnotes.

About the Author

Clint Bolick is director of the Goldwater Institute Center for Constitutional Litigation in Phoenix, Arizona, and serves of-counsel to the Rose Law Group in Scottsdale. One of America's leading constitutional litigators, Bolick was cofounder of the Institute for Justice, and in 2002 was recognized by *American Lawyer* as one of the three lawyers of the year for leading the nationwide legal defense of school choice programs. Bolick is a research fellow with the Hoover Institution and a 2006 recipient of the Bradley Prize. He recently published his first novel, *Nicki's Girl*.

Cato Institute

Founded in 1977, the Cato Institute is a public policy research foundation dedicated to broadening the parameters of policy debate to allow consideration of more options that are consistent with the traditional American principles of limited government, individual liberty, and peace. To that end, the Institute strives to achieve greater involvement of the intelligent, concerned lay public in questions of policy and the proper role of government.

The Institute is named for *Cato's Letters*, libertarian pamphlets that were widely read in the American Colonies in the early 18th century and played a major role in laying the philosophical foundation for the American Revolution.

Despite the achievement of the nation's Founders, today virtually no aspect of life is free from government encroachment. A pervasive intolerance for individual rights is shown by government's arbitrary intrusions into private economic transactions and its disregard for civil liberties.

To counter that trend, the Cato Institute undertakes an extensive publications program that addresses the complete spectrum of policy issues. Books, monographs, and shorter studies are commissioned to examine the federal budget, Social Security, regulation, military spending, international trade, and myriad other issues. Major policy conferences are held throughout the year, from which papers are published thrice yearly in the *Cato Journal*. The Institute also publishes the quarterly magazine *Regulation*.

In order to maintain its independence, the Cato Institute accepts no government funding. Contributions are received from foundations, corporations, and individuals, and other revenue is generated from the sale of publications. The Institute is a nonprofit, tax-exempt, educational foundation under Section 501(c)3 of the Internal Revenue Code.

CATO INSTITUTE
1000 Massachusetts Ave., N.W.
Washington, D.C. 20001
www.cato.org